Lessons in Islamic Jurisprudence

RELATED TITLES FROM ONEWORLD

Speaking in God's Name: Islamic Law, Authority and Women, Khaled M. Abou El Fadl, ISBN 1-85168-262-7

Lessons in Islamic Jurisprudence

MUḤAMMAD BĀQIR AṢ-ṢADR

Translated and with an introduction by

ROY PARVIZ MOTTAHEDEH

ONEWORLD
OXFORD

To my Arab friends past and present, Albert Hourani, Charles Issawi, Jeanette Wakin, and so many others, who taught me so much and have so much more to teach me.

LESSONS IN ISLAMIC JURISPRUDENCE

Oneworld Publications
(Sales and Editorial)
185 Banbury Road
Oxford OX2 7AR
England
www.oneworld-publications.com

Reprinted in paperback 2005
Original Arabic version
Muḥammad Bāqir al-Ṣadr, *Durūs fī ʿIlm al-Uṣūl*,
Beirut: Dār al-Kitāb al-Lubnānī, 1978

A CIP record for this title is available
from the British Library

ISBN 1-85168-324-0

Cover design and typesetting by Saxon Graphics Ltd, Derby, UK
Printed and bound in the USA by McNaughton & Gunn

Produced in association with the Harvard Center for Middle Eastern Studies

Contents

Preface

Over six years ago a Shī'ī businessman who knew of my continuing interest in Islamic and, in particular, Shī'ī jurisprudence commissioned me to translate the first volume of Muḥammad Bāqir aṣ-Ṣadr's survey of Islamic jurisprudence. At that time I immediately prepared a translation which I considered accurate but which was almost entirely unintelligible to the intelligent lay reader. I felt both the poverty of my own understanding of the subject and the nearly complete absence of suitable received terms in English.

In the following five years, I read in Western jurisprudence and the secondary literature on Islamic jurisprudence. While I failed to gain anything like a thorough knowledge of either field, I did finally decide that my improved translation had become a work that I could offer to the public. Alongside this translation I have provided an introduction intended to give the general reader enough background to place Ṣadr's work in the legal and juisprudential context to which it belongs. Yet I still feel that the book is an orphan. It exists without proper relatives partly because virtually no other translation of such a work exists and partly because it should be accompanied by another separate book discussing Shī'ī jurisprudence more extensively, both in terms of its relation with Islamic law and of its relation with

Western jurisprudence. If I am favored with a long life and the ability to read more deeply in these fields, I hope to write the companion book that is needed.

The problem of terminology to which I referred above carries with it inescapable dangers. Literal translation is sometimes extremely misleading. For example, my dear friend, the late Dr. Jeanette Wakin of Columbia, suggested that I render the word *khiṭāb* as "divine address." While this translation correctly captures the root idea of God's speech directed in the second person to mankind, it also seems to suggest the existence of a divine e-mail address, something we all hope for but are unlikely to find. English technical legal terms are also a danger. Although there are established translation terms for many of these English words in modern Arabic they often do not correspond to pre-modern usage. The term *waḍʿī* means "positive" in modern legal Arabic and a fine contemporary American interpreter of Islamic law has written an interpretion of the work of a pre-modern Muslim jurist in which he consistently translates this term as "positive." But as a result he at times severely distorts the meaning of the original. Nevertheless, when terms are reasonably close to those of Western law, as with "prima facie" in this translation, I feel comfortable using them, as long as there is a glossary that makes their original meaning in Islamic law quite clear. I have also adopted two terms from philosophy, "performative" and "assent," which, when glossed, seem to me to serve well. In some cases, I have introduced entirely new usages.

I have tried to be consistent in the use of all technical terms. These terms are given in bold type the first time they occur in the text. The reader can find the Arabic equivalents of all technical terms in the Glossary. There is also an index from Arabic to English. I believe the text of this book is more intelligible as a result of the consistency in the rendering of technical terms. If the book makes no other contribution to the field, it will at least have suggested some ways to make the study of Islamic jurisprudential thought more tractable for the non-specialist English reader.

Muḥammad Bāqir aṣ-Ṣadr's *Lessons in Islamic Jurisprudence* is a modern book. Nevertheless I feel certain that anyone who has mastered it will have a leg up in reading the extraordinarily rich tradition of pre-modern Islamic jurisprudential literature. The Arabic text of this book is readily available. My analytical summary on pages 145 to 172 is to some degree a commentary as well as a summary and may help the reader in following the text.

* * *

I am truly grateful to the many people who have made this book possible. Early on I received encouragement in my studies of jurisprudence from a distinguished lawyer friend, Dr. Saud Shawwaf. Over the years I have depended upon the intellectual assistance of Professor Hossein Modarressi of Princeton University, who has so generously given his time to educate me. I appreciate the learned comments on the translation by Dr. Aron Zysow. I also want to thank Professor Ridwan al-Sayyid of the University of Beirut, Dr. Abd-al-Karim Soroush, Kristen Stilt and Waheed Hussain for their valuable and important comments on the Introduction. Thanks are also due to Catherine Hall, who created the index.

It is, however, to my friend of forty years, John H. McCloskey, that I owe the most for his help in the final stages of preparing the manuscript, when my inability to type or to maintain any sort of organization almost defeated me.

Introduction

Muḥammad Bāqir aṣ-Ṣadr, one of whose works on Islamic **jurisprudence** is translated here, is among the leading modern thinkers in this field. This introduction seeks to locate his work for the intelligent lay reader by offering: a discussion of the nature of Islamic law; a discussion of the nature of Islamic jurisprudence; a discussion of the relation of this system of jurisprudence to Roman and canon law; and a very brief sketch of the life of the author.

The Nature of Islamic Law

It was by no means inevitable that law should have become so central to higher learning among most Muslims in the pre-modern period. For over a thousand years the great majority of Muslim jurists agreed that out of over six thousand verses in the Qur'ān there were only five hundred verses with legal content. Most of the "legal" verses concern *'ibādāt*, approximately "acts of devotion," such as prayer and the pilgrimage. Out of these five hundred verses, there are about one hundred and ninety that deal with non-ritual aspects of the law; only matters of inheritance are laid out in any detail.

As to why legal culture became central to so many Muslims in subsequent centuries, I can give only a partial answer. The Qur'ān, according to one very widely accepted reading, by its spirit encourages legal culture since it speaks repeatedly of the *ḥudūd*, literally "the limits" or "boundaries." In the Qur'ān this word does not mean "the prescribed punishments," as it came to mean in later Islamic law, but "the limits" which circumscribe good behavior; and in almost all instances *ḥudūd* in the Qur'ān is best translated as "laws." For example, in a verse on divorce (and most mentions of "the limits" are in passages on divorce and fasting), the Qur'ān reads, "... these are the laws [*ḥudūd*] of God: do not transgress them. Those who transgress them are unjust (or 'oppressive')." (II: 229). Another verse on divorce says, "... these are the laws of God. One who transgresses [literally, "passes beyond them"] has done injustice [or "acts oppressively"] to him or herself ..." (LXV: 2). In earlier centuries the study of Islamic law was called "the laws/limits and the knowledge [of them]," *al-ḥudūd wa-l-'ilm*, or simply the "knowledge" (*al-'ilm*). And indeed the Qur'ān connects laws and knowledge, in a verse which ends, "...and these are the laws [*ḥudūd*] of God; he makes them clear [*yubayyinu-hā*] to a people who understand/know [*ya'lamūna*, from the same root as *al-'ilm*]." (II: 230).

The Qur'ān also offers a number of statements specifying that certain things are "permitted" (*ḥalāl*) or "forbidden" (*ḥarām*). Therefore, given that there were some "laws" specifically laid down and some things actually classified as "permitted" or "forbidden," and given that Muslims were in touch with three powerful legal systems, the Roman, the Jewish, and the Sassanian Persian, is it surprising that legally minded Muslims felt it necessary to go beyond the brief treatment of the law in the Qur'ān to develop a fully fledged legal system?

Yet as this system developed it became clear that it was something grander than law: it aspired to classify and categorize all human acts. Later jurists summarized this ambition in a maxim that said, "In the presence of God there is a **ruling** or 'classification' (*ḥukm*) for every instance of human behavior." The jurists saw it as their responsibility (and, to some extent, that of every human being) to **derive**, from what they believed to be potential **sources of the law**, the most likely classification or categorization of any human act in the eyes of God. He is "the Lord of the Day of Reckoning," as the Qur'ān repeatedly says, and it was considered essential to know how He would reckon the deeds of one's life, even when they were neither "forbidden" nor "obligatory." After long dispute the jurists came to agree on five "predicates" appropriate for any legal proposition expressing the ruling (*ḥukm*) which evaluates a human act in moral terms. An act is either "forbidden," "discouraged," "permissible" (meaning free of any moral weight), "recommended," or "mandatory." Normally only the "forbidden" and, in some cases, the "mandatory," could be matters for consideration in an Islamic court, and only these matters would be called "law" according to a widespread Anglo-American tradition. But it should be understood that the so-called manuals of Islamic law would be considerably slighter if they contained only matters enforceable by courts. Islamic law proper is embedded in a moral hermeneutic, or system of interpretation. It can be argued that even in the Anglo-American system we have laws such as tax laws, the object of which is to encourage or discourage certain types of behavior in areas such as personal savings and home ownership, which are of course legally optional. To give another example, "Good Samaritan" laws encourage help to the distressed in cases of emergency by reducing liability to the rescuer.

The **jurists** understand the middle category, "permissible" or "morally neutral," to be central to the nature of the law. "The legal **presumption** concerning things is their permissibility (*'ibāḥa*)," as the famous maxim says. This word can be translated "license," from which point of view the need for "limits" is clear. It can also be understood as "liberty," and a person's fundamental liberty to act as she or he wishes in the world has been an important concept to many Muslim reformers. Some moral philosophers in the contemporary West consider such a presumption necessary to any system of ethics.

A kindred concept is "the presupposition of innocence," which partly overlaps with the Anglo-American presumption of innocence. When born, every person's legal standing (*dhimma*) is innocent/free of guilt (*barī'*). This presupposition is seen as self-evident; for the accused in a law case is innocent until evidence (*bayyina*) is brought to prove otherwise, and the newborn is not yet responsible for any acts whatsoever.

The Historical Development of Islamic Law

The above account of the way in which Islamic law developed is too stylized to be fully historical; it represents the attempts of later jurists to tidy up the history of a very lively intellectual debate which, like any other such formative episode, was filled with disagreement and took place under the pressure of real concerns. Fortunately, a fair amount of material on these early debates survives. (It is one of the merciful aspects of Islamic law that its extended treatments carry the history of virtually all opinions of previous jurists of any importance into later works, a display of learning that allows the author to show that he has considered discarded opinions, as well as – on rare occasions – to adopt an earlier opinion.)

It would seem both from the Qur'ān and its commentaries that many of these early debates had to do with the way in which Islamic law should understand itself over and against other law or laws. Verses 42 through 50 of Surah V (*al-Mā'ida*) are held by most Muslim biographies of the Prophet to relate to an incident (supposed by Muslim commentators to have occurred in the fifth year of the Prophet's authority in Medina) when some of the Medinese Jews came to the Prophet asking him to arbitrate among them. In verse 44 the Prophet is told, "In truth we have revealed the Torah in which is guidance and light, by which the Prophets who submitted to God judged the Jews; and the rabbis and sages judged by such of God's Book as they were bidden to observe … ." Verse 48 goes on to explain that God has revealed laws for each community, "To each of you we have given a law and a way. Had God wished it He would have made you a single [legal] community (*'umma*) ... ." (This divinely willed legal plurality was, of course, why Muslims generally tolerated religious communities founded before the coming of Islam. They always had the option of considering these communities as "pagans," a category of persons that the Qur'ān and the Prophet did not tolerate within Arabia. Until very recently religions founded after the coming of Islam were not legally recognized.)[1]

The expansion of Muslim rule brought legal questions that had to be sorted out immediately, and the Islamic legal tradition would later consider the decisions on these legal questions to be an exercise in **ijtihād**, the effort to derive rulings from their proper sources. 'Umar, the second caliph (from 13 A.H./634 A.D. to 23 A.H./644 A.D.) had to choose between precedents. The Prophet had made different arrangements with different Jewish and Christian communities in Arabia. In one instance he arranged for an annual poll tax, in another, the Christian community of Najrān agreed to send two thousand robes to Medina each year. How by extension from such precedents could a ruling be established for the taxation of other Christian and Jewish communities? There was also the problem of the status of the land in the large empire suddenly acquired by the Muslims during the reign of 'Umar. The jurist 'Abū Yūsūf in his book on the land tax tells us that Bilāl, the famous Ethiopian companion of the Prophet, told 'Umar, "Divide the lands among those who conquer them, just as the spoils of the army are divided [on the battlefield]." But 'Umar refused, saying, "God has given a share in these lands to those who shall come after you." As in the question of taxation there were mixed precedents, and for the next century opposition to 'Umar's decision to give the tax revenue and title of the conquered land to the "treasury of the Muslims" remained controversial and a cause for serious revolts.[2]

While the first four caliphs had an enormous share in making the decisions which would become law, their successors, the dynasty of Umayyad caliphs, continued to promulgate their own rulings as binding legal decisions for matters as various as marriage, the law of sale, and blood-money. The well-known "fiscal rescript" written by 'Umar II (caliph from 99 A.H./717 A.D. to 101 A.H./720 A.D.), usually counted as the most pious of the Umayyads, shows this caliph ruling on the tax status of converts and kindred matters. Even subordinate Umayyad officials could make rulings which might find subsequent authority in the law. When an Arab general invaded the province of Sind in 93/711, he recognized Hindus as protected people like the Christians and Jews, and the majority of later Muslim jurists of the Ḥanafī school, the Sunni school predominant in South Asia, recognized this ruling.

Gradually the caliphs lost the power to make legal rulings. Yet they retained until the very end the theoretical authority to appoint judges and to hold their own court, the *maẓālim*, or court to judge "contraventions of justice." The jurisdiction of this court was very wide. Although in theory there is no appeal from the ruling of a qadi, in practice cases were appealed to the *maẓālim* court. Moreover, it functioned as an important court of appeal from decisions in administrative law and against the misbehavior of administrators, matters with which most qadis were unwilling to deal. Yet the *maẓālim* jurisdiction never reached out to the masses who lived under the caliph's rule; it did not, for example, develop "delegated" judges, as the qadis did in order to have sitting judges in remote towns. The *maẓālim* remained an active but idiosyncratic expression of the ruler's desire to be seen personally as the last resort in the search for justice.

The authority of the Umayyad caliphs to make law or even in any way to govern had been challenged from the start, in significant part by the "Partisans" or Shī'a, of 'Alī ibn 'Abī Ṭālib the first cousin and son-in-law of the Prophet, and some of these Shī'īs felt that 'Alī had been explicitly appointed by the Prophet as his successor. The Kharijites, in contrast, opposed both 'Alī and the Umayyads because they had all committed "sins" and the Kharijites would accept no sinful ruler. (The 'Ibāḍīs, descended from one branch of the Kharijites, and now to be found principally in Uman and North Africa, have their own school of law.) The pious opposition to the

Umayyads not only shrank the caliph's authority to promulgate legal rulings, it also created a number of circles in which a more intense discussion of religious matters took place, and their members were the forerunners of the ulema, the specialists in religious learning so prominent in the later Islamic Middle East.

'Abū Ḥanīfa (d. 150/767) was both prominent in and typical of these circles. He is accounted the founder of the Ḥanafī school of law named after him, although how much 'Abū Ḥanīfa was a Ḥanafī is far from clear. One story – very possibly a legend – has an Umayyad governor flog him for refusing appointment as a qadi. It seems without question that he supported the political claims of the family of 'Alī. He died in prison in Baghdad, the capital of the 'Abbasids, the dynasty of caliphs that succeeded the Umayyads. The lifestory of this great early jurist and theologian as constructed from reliable historical accounts and legend shows a suspicion of association with government which would persist among the ulema of the Middle East. It also shows a gap between judges and jurists that would last. Some learned men did become judges, but usually the most learned jurists shunned judgeships. Nevertheless, the practical experience of the judges fed legal thinking in that the decisions of judges were sometimes challenged by the jurists and sometimes ably defended by the judges in circles that met to discuss the law. Ibn 'Abī Laylā, the judge for Kufa in 'Abū Ḥanīfa's time, tried – largely unsuccessfully – to establish the legal basis for his judgments against the opinion of his more able contemporary, 'Abū Ḥanīfa. But the practical nature of Ibn 'Abī Laylā's opinions is said to have given some of them lasting value as against 'Abū Ḥanīfa's more theoretical approach, dictated by the latter's search for consistency.[3]

The distance between the "pious opposition" and government also accounts for the development of the independent *fatwā*, or opinion, so similar to the *responsa* which exist in Roman and Jewish law. Conscientious Muslims went to the legally minded among the forerunners of the ulema and got opinions, including opinions on matters not ordinarily dealt with by courts. The Umayyad state, aware of this interest, appointed *muftīs*, givers of *responsa*, somewhat similar to the jurisconsults in the Roman system. Although later dynasties often appointed *muftīs*, many *muftīs* sought to remain and succeeded in remaining largely independent because people were free to choose their authorities and because a *muftī* who kept his distance from the government gained prestige among ordinary Muslims. The independence of the *muftī* was a significant part of the formation and persistence of a semi-independent community of jurists.

In time these communities of legal thinking developed regional differences. Mālik ibn 'Anas (d. 179/796), often called simply "the **Imam** of Medina," was the most able member in his generation among the circles that discussed Islamic law in Medina. The Medinese tradition considered itself continuous with the tradition of the Prophet, who spent the last ten years of his life there. It was assumed, reasonably enough, that the Prophet would have disapproved of Medinese customs not consonant with Islam, and therefore what survived in "the practice of Medina" had been expressly or tacitly approved. Hence, in Medina in Mālik's time, while the quantity and quality of something sold usually had to be known for the sale to be valid, the very practical Medinese custom of exchanging an inexactly known quantity of ripe dates on a tree for dried dates was allowed and became part of the tradition of the Mālikī school of law (and subsequently of other schools). Mālik, by the way, was also very concerned with the classification of rulings and Prophetic sayings and not merely in Medinese traditions. In early books on law Mālik's school is often called "the school of Medina," and 'Abū Ḥanīfa's school "the school of Kufa," which represents the understanding that these were in fact regional schools although in the homes of all these schools there was a variety of opinion.

It was also in Medina that two of the Imams of the Twelver Shī'īs, Muḥammad al-Bāqir (d. sometime between 114/732 and 118/736) and his son Ja'far aṣ-Ṣādiq (d. 148/765), made a significant contribution to Islamic law in general as well as developing a more specifically Shī'ī school of law. Muḥammad al-Bāqir's disciples included prominent Sunnis such as al-'Awzā'ī and 'Abū Ḥanīfa, both founders of law schools. Muḥammad al-Bāqir's legal views were written down by his circle and passed into Shī'ī law. Ja'far aṣ-Ṣādiq held an even higher position of respect and prominence in legal discussion among Muslims in general and both he and his father are counted as reliable transmitters of **ḥadīth** among Sunnis. Ja'far aṣ-Ṣādiq gave a very large number of legal rulings which served to orient the Shī'ī tradition.

Another source for regional difference was the pre-Islamic underlay of regional schools. The influence of this underlay is downplayed in many Muslim accounts of the development of Islamic law, but unnecessarily so. The Prophet during his "farewell" pilgrimage in 10/632 carefully went through the rituals of the pilgrimage, understood to have been established by Abraham, and made clear both in action and description what was authentic and what was unacceptable pagan accretion. This method of developing the law is called "confirmation" (*taqrīr*) by the jurists, and it is supported by the first part of one of the verses already cited. Verse 48 of the fifth Surah of the Qur'ān begins, "We have revealed to you the Book in truth [or, "with the truth"], confirming [*muṣaddiqan*] that Scripture which already exists … ." In a widely respected letter ascribed to 'Alī ibn 'Abī Ṭālib and written as instructions to Mālik al-'Ashtar, his appointee as governor of Egypt, we read, "Abolish no proper custom [*sunna*] which has been enacted by their [the Egyptians'] leaders, through which harmony has been strengthened and because of which the subjects have prospered. Create no new custom which might in any way prejudice the customs of the past, lest reward for them belong to him who originated them, and the burden be upon you to the extent that you have abolished them."[4]

Yet the desire to see Islamic law as a separate system over and against earlier systems outweighed the interest in carefully recording when "confirmation" took place after the Prophet's death. Christians, who at first had little reason to think they should develop a legal system, soon created a whole system of bishops' courts, then took and triumphantly reshaped Roman law to their own ends. A fair number of the axioms which were central to Roman law are to be found in Islamic law. Even if these maxims are present not because of borrowing but because of the common conclusions of developed law, isn't their presence a confirmation that other legal systems strove to achieve the same goals as did Islamic law? And yet, unnecessarily, the traditional narrative of Islamic law allowed little place for interest in continuities and parallels.

In any case, it is clear that Islamic law was overwhelmingly jurist-made law; and by the second half of the second/eighth century full-fledged jurists emerged. In the case of Muḥammad ibn 'Idrīs ash-Shāfi'i (d. 204/820), usually called al-'Imām ash-Shāfi'ī, we have not only a powerful jurist but also, according to later Muslim tradition, the founder of jurisprudence, the discipline of **deriving** law from its proper and appropriate "roots" or **sources** (*'uṣūl al-fiqh*). It should be noted that Shāfi'ī, like Mālik and 'Abū Ḥanīfa, was at one time a partisan of the 'Alid cause.

In his celebrated *Epistle* he attempted, as an historian of the subject says, "a systematization, a codification, and, up to a point, a rationalization of understanding the Law."[5] It is Shāfi'ī who clarifies that the subject of the law is the legally capable individual considered as someone who is subject to moral obligation (*mukallaf*, **legal agent**), and that for every act there is a ruling (*ḥukm*). He discusses the need to rank in order of priority the "roots" or foundations of the law and the need to systematize analogical reasoning (*qiyās*). In making the **Sunna** (which means, among other things, the "practice" of the Prophet) a proper **source** (*'aṣl*) alongside the Qur'ān, he stipulated that the jurist is to accept only a properly established **account** (*ḥadīth*, *khabar*) about what the Prophet said, did, or gave tacit assent to, to the exclusion of mere local tradition, which his teacher Mālik had accepted. His insistence on a strict study of **analogy** was a rejection of the freer forms of legal reasons such as commonweal, to which 'Abū Ḥanīfa had frequent recourse. In short, he sought to rein in the various schools of Islamic law, partly in a traditionalist direction, in that he set scriptural **prooftext** so far ahead of other sources of law, and partly in an innovative direction, with his demand that legal **arguments** be justified and (as in the case of analogy) be well developed.

It was too late. The substantive law (that is, the law as written down by specific jurists with the intention that it be generally adopted) was already too developed, and the existing schools too conscious of their tradition, to yield to the challenge of the new rules proposed by Shāfiʿī. For a century Shāfiʿī's *Epistle* remained without progeny. But when jurists turned to writing jurisprudence, the sophistication of Shāfiʿī's program was an overwhelming influence and eventually all the law schools wanted to represent themselves as fitting into some form of Shāfiʿī's system. We will return to the development of jurisprudential writing below.

Shāfiʿī demanded that *ḥadīth* or *khabar*, narratives as to what the Prophet did and said and tacitly assented to, be properly accredited. In this demand he was at the forefront of a movement for *ḥadīth* criticism which resulted in the writing of "canonical" *ḥadīth* books in the third/ninth century among the Sunnis (and in the fourth/tenth and fifth/eleventh centuries among the Twelver Shīʿīs). Although it took centuries to achieve near-consensus as to which *ḥadīth* collections were canonical, two achieved instant recognition among Sunnis, those of al-Bukhārī (d. 256/870) and Muslim ibn al-Ḥajjāj (d. 261/817). Both aimed to present only such *ḥadīth* as had a reliable **chain** of transmitters extending back to the Prophet. (*Ḥadīth* rather confusingly was used for a single narrative or as a collective plural.) To be reliable, a transmitter had to be known to be of good character and likely to have met both the preceding and succeeding links in the chain. Many early scholars had presented *ḥadīth* with "imperfect" chains of transmission or even without any chains. Non-Muslim scholars (and recently some Muslim scholars) have suggested that a fair body of *ḥadīth* acquired its Prophetic pedigree in the century and a half before the "canonical" books appeared. In any case, even the collections of Bukhārī and Muslim ibn al-Ḥajjāj have *ḥadīth*s with incomplete chains of transmitters. By their arrangement of chapters Bukhārī and Muslim show the growing concern of the jurists for reliable legal material, as both use sub-headings somewhat similar to those of the law books.

Throughout the centuries there has been a dispute about the standing of accounts that did not come down through **wide-scale transmission**, but from a small number – even a single – line of reliable transmitters. Some of these *ḥadīth* are constantly invoked in the law books. For example, the *ḥadīth* that says: "The believers must fulfill the lawful conditions in [their contracts] (*al-mu'minūn 'inda shurūṭihim*)" is such a "solitary" or "idiosyncratic" *ḥadīth*, even though it is continually invoked in the chapters on sale in the law books. Some of the "idiosyncratic" *ḥadīth*s were too important to the law to be shoved overboard. Ibn aṣ-Ṣalāḥ ash-Shahrazūrī (d. 643/1245) in his introduction to the *ḥadīth* sciences, still considered the most authoritative book on this subject, points out that if wide-scale transmission demands transmission from a large number of the Companions of the Prophet as well as multiple transmitters in later generations, then only one *ḥadīth* of the many hundreds of thousands in existence would qualify.[6]

Ḥadīth came to rank with the Qur'ān as a source of law. The *ḥadīth* was treated according to the rules developed by the Qur'ān commentators for dealing with the seeming contradictions between Qur'ān verses. Some verses in the Qur'ān, for instance, allow the drinking of wine; but one forbids it. The commentators tried to establish when each verse was revealed. From this chronological framework one could determine that prohibition of wine-drinking came later and "abrogated" the verse permitting wine-drinking. Correspondingly, there were abrogated and abrogating *ḥadīth*.

The virtually equal status of reliable *ḥadīth* was a boon to the jurists, who had so little law from the Qur'ān alone; but it created intellectual problems. Whereas the text of the Qur'ān was fixed (except as to minor and clearly established questions such as different pronunciations of certain words), the scholars of *ḥadīth* accepted as equally sound reliably transmitted *ḥadīth*s with the same meaning but different wording. (Strangely, other textual criticism of the *ḥadīth* was limited; it was not a subject for concern in *ḥadīth*-criticism that the *ḥadīth* foretell "heretical" movements such as the Murji'ites and Kharijites of the early period but do not foretell later heresies.) The standing of sound *ḥadīth*s, which collectively describe the Sunna, or practice of the Prophet, was so high that some jurists held that the Sunna could abrogate the Qur'ān.

In the fourth/tenth century the book market, agreement within schools of law, and the needs of students and judges called forth manuals of law, some of which have kept their standing until the present. The pressure of the book market deserves more attention among historians of Islamic law. The great polymath al-Mas'ūdī (d. 345/956), for example, released his rambling (but entertaining) world histories in three lengths: a very long everything-I-know version, *'Akhbār az-Zamān* (lost but referred to in his other works); a work called the *Kitāb al-'Awsaṭ* ("Middle Book"), an abridgement of the long version, also lost; *Murūj adh-Dhahab* ("The Fields of Gold"), also a middle length version, which survives; and *Kitāb at-Tanbīh wal-'Ishrāf*, an abridgement and summary of the longer works. Books were expensive, and authors often preferred restating their subject at different lengths to revising old works. The same pattern has been followed by some jurists down to our own time.

The need of judges for a quick book to consult, of students for a smallish book to memorize (in what was a highly mnemonic culture) and the achievement of a large degree of agreement within the Mālikī school account for the popularity of the short *Epistle* by Ibn 'Abī Zayd al-Qayrawānī (d. 386/996), a book still memorized from the author's native Tunisia to Nigeria.

Qayrawānī's *Epistle* offers a concrete starting point to consider the way in which law changed. Discussing an important topic, the *ḥubūs* or *waqf*, the charitable trust or pious endowment, Qayrawānī in the *Epistle* speaks only of the trust set up for the family and descendants of the founder. The word refers to an institution in Tunisia, where the traditions of the Roman latifundia survived the Arab conquest and were threatened by the complicated divisions of inheritance among relatives required in the Qur'ān and well elaborated by the jurists. The *waqf*, literally the "stopping" of property from circulation, has no Qur'ānic basis except insofar as it fulfills the general exhortations in the Qur'ān to charity. The institution of the "pious trust" founded for non-familial interests exists in Qayrawānī's time even if he thought an elementary book in Māliki law need not discuss it.

If we turn to a Ḥanafi handbook of the Ottoman period, *ad-Durr al-Mukhtār* ("The Chosen Pearls") by al-Ḥaṣkafi (d. 1088 A.H./1677 A.D.), we find a discussion that has gained sophistication over the centuries. The author tells us that a waqf resembles a partnership in that the owner's property is inserted into someone else's property, i.e., God's. The author is aware that 'Abū Ḥanīfa, the eponym of the Ḥanafi school, thought that any charitable trust was revocable, whereas later Ḥanafis disagreed. Many aspects of the making and preserving of such trusts are discussed. For example, the objects legally appropriate to be made into charitable trusts are painstakingly defined. Here the author says (contrary to the opinion of most pre-Ottoman jurists) that cash can be the object of a dedication to a charitable trust, the cash-*waqf* that lent money at interest being a widespread institution in the Ottoman empire. Ḥaṣkafi also raises the interesting point that by the rules of analogy, it would be wrong to dedicate a Qur'ān (since it cannot be the object of a financial transaction, and one cannot dedicate as a *waqf* an object of no market value). But, Ḥaṣkafi says, the *ḥadīth* tells us, "What the Muslims see as right, is right in the eyes of God." This legal maxim was the justification for *istiḥsān*, "favorable construction," that is to say, a looser method of legal construction which sets aside the results of strict construction in favor of the common good. In many cases, the presence of '*urf* or "custom" is an occasion for the jurist to suspect that this **common usage** exists for the common good.

Some constant traits of the substantive law can be seen in these law books. By the fourth/tenth centuries it became customary to divide the law into "roots," which I have called jurisprudence, and substantive law, which was called the "branches" or *furū*ʿ. The phrase "substantive law" may give the mistaken impression that these law books were "codes." They were not, except for those rare cases in which the government promulgated some area of Islamic law in an official version. Many of these last books stand between an ideal world and a real world over which the jurist has limited influence but nevertheless the jurist wishes the believer to know that there is a practical, yet divinely ordained, path to follow. These books offered legal opinions as to what the law was. They were written within the tradition of a law school and that tradition rests heavily on the writer.

By the fifth/eleventh century it was clear that a certain amount of legal pluralism was here to stay. Some law schools, such as that of ʾAwzāʿī in Syria and Spain, would dwindle. But at least from the perspective of al-Māwardī (d. 450/1058), an extremely influential jurist in Baghdad, there were four legitimate law schools. This view would not find general acceptance until the seventh/thirteenth century when the Mamluk rulers of Egypt made the system of four schools truly and finally canonical. Ideas spread among the four Sunni schools as well as between them and the Twelver Shīʿīs, and the revolution started by Shāfiʿī was complete in the sense that Sunni and Shīʿī jurists shared a lot of the scaffolding language of jurisprudence, although this language was comparatively rare in the books on substantive law.

Books on the "differences" among great jurists, among the four law schools and between Sunnis and Twelver Shīʿīs are among the first legal texts preserved for us and this genre has continued to be cultivated right up to the present day. However, after a while this genre became rather stereotyped and seldom acted as a fulcrum by the use of which to raise new discussions in the law. Each law school developed relatively stable sub-headings under which things were discussed, most often adhering to the nodes around which legal discussion in that school had developed in the first place. For example, "contract" does not appear in the handbooks as a separate subject in any of the four Sunni schools or in the Twelver Shīʿī traditions, even though it is mentioned in the Qur'ān. The fullest discussion of it comes in the chapters on sales.

The founding of the madrasas or colleges gave a great push to the stabilization of the law. In early times teaching took place in the mosques and by the fourth/tenth century lectureships in mosques were endowed. But in the fifth/eleventh century the institution of the endowed school was brought from the northeastern area of Iran to Baghdad and beyond at the behest of the great vizier Niẓām al-Mulk (d. 485/1092) who served the Saljuqs, a dynasty whose empire encompassed almost all of Western Asia. Eventually the institution would spread to Morocco and China. Niẓām al-Mulk gave rich endowments for his madrasas, enough to house and feed their students. He also dictated their curriculum: their principal task was to teach Shāfiʿī law. (Niẓām al-Mulk himself accepted only one other school, the Ḥanafī, as legitimate, and considered it a very distant second.) The madrasas made sure that law was at the center of Islamic learning. Teaching other subjects such as rhetoric and mathematics, and even, in the case of the Shīʿīs, philosophy, was allowed in the madrasas, but these subjects were there under the half-true excuse that they aided legal study. In fact, they were kept in a subordinate place. Law's dominance of endowed higher education was a loss for many areas of learning. But the law curricula were similar enough to give a common language to the ulema, in general allowing them to recognize across law schools who were members of their club.

It must be remembered that the ulema were not in any way consecrated and had no sacerdotal function. To maintain their prestige and authority they had to have mastery of something not easily accessible to the average literate person. While accessible elementary legal texts continued to be taught, a whole new class of textbook, including texts on jurisprudence, were written. They aimed at so much concision that they became virtually unintelligible. The student would memorize the passage assigned for the day and possibly read a commentary. In class the teacher would explain the text with examples, and might end the lesson by saying, "And therefore we say: ..." at which time he and the students would recite the dehydrated original, which had by now sprung into its full form in the minds of the students. Later in the student's education these memorized passages were like pegs on which to hang the keys of things learned in further study of the subject. This method accounts in part for the long stability of the order in which chapters were presented in law books and other genres of madrasa books.

The Nature of Islamic Jurisprudence

The history of jurisprudence is narrower and less studied than substantive law and is often more difficult to discover. In a sense the tradition of jurisprudence began in the age of the Prophet when, according to *ḥadīth*, he was asked questions and sometimes explained his answers, or when, as in *ḥadīth* given by Ḥaṣkafi, he gave general principles of interpretation. This discussion on these topics continued to flourish after the Prophet and took a great leap forward with the work of Shāfi'ī. But would he have counted his book as jurisprudence, as later scholars did? The *Epistle* of al-Qayrawānī begins with a little theology and jurisprudence, but is mostly a book on substantive law. It was only in the course of fourth/tenth and fifth/eleventh centuries that jurisprudence emerged as a genre and its independent position was clarified.

Fiqh (literally "discernment") is a human attempt at knowing the *Sharī'a*, the divinely ordained "path" which only God knows perfectly. The word *Sharī'a* shines more brightly and is seen more reverentially than *fiqh*. Nevertheless, it is essential for the *fiqh* to be known on the human plane as accurately as possible. A method of explaining texts gains authority as it gains internal consistency and agrees with theological ideas. Do commonweal arguments, so favored by 'Abū Ḥanīfa, have as much strength as arguments from scripture or by analogy? What are the presuppositions of the law? How can the linguistic disciplines tell us when commands in the Qur'ān are metaphorical? What were the qualifications for carrying out *ijtihād*, the independent effort at legal reasoning?

To this last question there developed a partial answer: one must be trained in jurisprudence as well as in substantive law. Just as the discipline of jurisprudence was coming into its own, the madrasas were founded and jurisprudence was adopted into the madrasa curriculum. If one wanted to be a truly first-rate jurist, he should have some training in jurisprudence. The books on substantive law reveled in discussing difficult questions and seeming contradictions in the law; jurisprudence provided a means to answer them in an ever subtler way.

Jurisprudence was the threshold between law and theology, which was often called *'uṣūl ad-dīn*, the "roots of religion" just as jurisprudence was "the roots of law." It was assumed that before coming to the law a Muslim had found reasons to believe in God, the Qur'ān, and the exemplary life of the Prophet. Theology, which deals with these issues, also dealt with questions such as free will and predestination, which inevitably occur in a monotheistic system. But Islamic theology also deals with some topics more prominent among Muslim than Christian thinkers. If God speaks to man directly in the second person in the Qur'ān, what is the nature of that speech? On this issue there were many schools of thought, only two of which are discussed here. The speech included "commands," often in the **imperative**, and "prohibitions." For one school the speech of God was literally true; that is, when the Qur'ān says, "The All-Merciful sat firmly upon the throne," it meant that God literally sat on His throne. Some softened this formula by saying that one should believe without asking "how" (that is, in what sense this language is to be understood). Similarly the commands and prohibitions in both the Qur'ān and sound *ḥadīth* were to be literally obeyed. This approach to the text of the Qur'ān existed (with some variation) among Muslims from an early period and still exists; its partisans are sometimes called *'Ahl al-Ḥadīth*. Such literalist views resemble Christian fundamentalism and many (but not all) groups labeled fundamentalist in the Muslim world at present are literalist in this original sense.

An opposing stance was taken by the Mu'tazilite school. This school had almost as many branches as it had members. The branch associated with the Basran 'Abū l-Hudhayl (d. *c.*227/840) is discussed here. He vehemently opposed anthropomorphism and saw the **literal** acceptance of statements such as "The All-Merciful sat firmly on His throne" as contrary to the absolute transcendence of God above His creatures. God is one; He has no form or limit. God is all-knowing and all-seeing, etc., but His knowledge is identical with Himself. A human is responsible for his/her actions. God's speech, including the Qur'ān, is created by God.

The justice of God meant that certain of His laws could be found by reason alone, although the most correct form of these laws and of the way to fulfill them (such as how to worship Him), could be found only through revelation. They therefore adopted the categories "good/beautiful" (*ḥasan*) and "bad/ugly" (*qabīḥ*) as determinable by the "intellect/reason" (*'aql*) whereas the "mandatory" (*wājib*) can be determined by revelation alone. This system resembles Hellenistic theories of natural law with which the Mu'tazilites were acquainted. The intellectual rigor that Mu'tazilites introduced into theological discussion commanded respect even among their opponents and influenced all the major schools of theology among Muslims. Its influence on the Karaite "heresy" in Judaism is also well-known.

The major school rejecting Mu'tazilism was founded by al-'Ash'arī (d. 324/935), who was a former Mu'tazilite, and who, for all his great achievement and undoubted originality, uses many of the techniques of argumentation used by the Mu'tazilites. 'Ash'arism formed a more coherent school than Mu'tazilism but its followers were by no means in complete agreement. Of course 'Ash'arī accepted that God is just, but God's omnipotence can not be contained; if He is just, it is because He chooses to be just; and we have no business asking whether His commands are just. 'Ash'arism offered a "strong" theory in that it did not appear to compromise the omnipotence of God in any way. (At times 'Ash'arism seems close to certain versions of Protestant theology.) It makes Islamic law "positive" law in the sense that God alone, freed of all constraints, posits it. But to strip goodness and continuity of all rational justification had some problems of which the 'Ash'arites were aware. The perception of the "customary" behavior of things – the 'Ash'arite formula used to replace natural law in both the physical and moral world – required reason, both inductive and deductive. To carry out analogies – a practice fully accepted by 'Ash'arīs – required reasoning. Moreover, there had been a broad consensus since the third/ninth century that the "right" was "good," a view that the 'Ash'aris generally accepted. It was explained by them in ingenious – but to this author not wholly successful – ways.

Eventually Sunnis rejected the theories of the Mu'tazilites, while the Twelver and Zaydī Shī'is accepted a large part of them, often in the version developed by 'Abū al-Hudhayl. Accompanying this parting of ways was a parting of ways in the role given to reason/intellect. For Sunnis there are rational presuppositions such as the use of reason in interpretation of the sources of the law. There is also analogy, one of the four major sources of Sunni law, since analogy requires reasoning in its application (although many Sunnis believe the validity of analogy comes only from its validation by the words of Prophetic *ḥadīth*).

Shī'is, on the contrary, embrace reason/intellect as one of their four major sources. They reject analogy, however, on the grounds that it sometimes yields too many possibilities. Is smoking prohibited by analogy with the prohibition of wine? It depends on a guess as to what is the explanatory principle for the prohibition of wine: its ability to make someone drunk, or because of some other psychotropic effect. Hence a disagreement on the permissibility of smoking. (One long dead Sunni school said that only what was explicitly forbidden was forbidden; God had forbidden wine, not beer, and we have no business guessing His motives.)

The Shī'ī acceptance of Mu'tazilism was signaled by their adoption of a Mu'tazilite slogan, "Everything that reason ordains, **divine law** ordains" (and, it is understood to be implied, vice-versa).

As Muḥammad Bāqir aṣ-Ṣādr said in another work, this program was never actually carried out by a Shī'ī jurist.[7] But the theoretical and, in some cases, the actual importance of intellect and natural law is everywhere present in Shī'ī jurisprudence. Shī'īs, for example, enthusiastically adopted Aristotelian logic and used the syllogism instead of analogy (although later Sunni jurists came to approve some figures of the syllogism). Muḥammad Bāqir aṣ-Ṣādr in the book translated here, without distorting Shī'ī law, tries to emphasize its (genuine) scriptural basis, partly to counter the Sunni critique of Shī'ism as too inclined to appeal to reason. It is striking that the theory of obligation which logically should stand at the opening of the book actually stands two-thirds of the way through it in the discussion of **procedural principles**.

Shi'ism went through a conservative phase, in which a group of Shī'ī jurists called 'Akhbārīs insisted on the primacy of the accounts (*'akhbār*) of **infallible persons**. They held that everyone with a good knowledge of Arabic, the Qur'ān, and these accounts, the points of **consensus** among the Shī'īs, and the proper use of the rational argument (*dalīl 'aqlī*) could find the ruling appropriate to any case. Note that Shī'ī law even in this conservative phase did not completely reject intellect.

In the thirteenth/nineteenth century the 'Uṣūlī school in Shī'ī law roundly won the high ground for the claims of intellect (and also for the special position of the jurists). 'Akhbārīs survive only in a few remote outposts. The decisive blows in this battle were dealt by the saintly Murtaḍā al-'Anṣārī (d. 1281/1864), who vastly extended the use of the procedural principles discussed by Ṣadr toward the end of the book. The placement of consideration of these principles at the end of his text is no measure of their use in the past century and a half, in which they have dominated many legal discussions. All of these procedural principles are based on intellect and Shī'ī jurisprudence reflects this change, although Ṣadr leaves most of his discussion of them for the second volume, not translated here. One of Ṣadr's most original works is entitled "The logical bases of induction" and is an attempt (deemed important but not wholly successful) to give a larger role to inductive reasoning in Islamic higher learning.

Jurisprudence was a threshold which led not only from theology to law but from law to theology. Modern Shīʿī law with its interest in principles with a rational basis has encouraged the traffic between the two areas.

One aspect of Shīʿī jurisprudence has been badly misrepresented in some Western books, which say that Shiʿism rejects the principle of consensus. It is true that Sunni consensus includes all Muslims or all Sunni jurists whereas Shīʿī consensus is achieved between either all Muslims or all Shīʿī jurists. But both traditions are concerned with fidelity to the actual general practice of Muslims, presumed, as in the Prophet's confirmation of the pilgrimage, to be preserved in its correct form because of the continuing concern of generation after generation of Muslims. Ritual law in particular is a great river of shared experience that runs down the history of the Muslims. Moreover, within the law schools there was concern to preserve the integrity of the school tradition. In this sense, although Islamic law did not formally accept the idea of precedent, the law books in practice heavily favored precedent.

How well did jurisprudence account for the substantive law? Jurisprudence made a brave attempt, but when jurisprudence came along, too much substantive law already existed for any theory to account for all of it. In fact, there was a very minor genre of works in which the specialist in jurisprudence attempted to prove the harmony between the "roots" and "branches," but such attempts were curiosities, not fully successful.

Nevertheless, once it was established, jurisprudence disciplined the jurists, and therefore exercised a centripetal influence. I have described the way in which Shāfiʿī wanted to bring both the Kufan and Medinese school under a common standard, and this impulse remained an important part of jurisprudence. It also, as discussed above, corresponded with the formation of the ulema as a self-conscious group, who would have destroyed their own authority if centrifugal forces had been allowed to operate.

It is a curiosity that jurisprudence did not take on two related topics, the "moral ends" of the law (*maqāṣid*) and the "norms" (*qawā'id*) of the law. Ḥanafi jurisprudence sometimes discussed a category literally called "cause" (*sabab*) which, if developed, might have constituted a deeper level of rational explanation than did the search for the connecting link of an analogy. A small genre on the moral ends of the law existed but was seldom integrated into jurisprudence. Although the "norms," often given in the forms of maxims, seem very central to the way jurists think, and are occasionally cited in the books on jurisprudence, before the nineteenth century, they were never, it would seem, central to the construction of any jurisprudential theory. They too were treated in a separate genre. There seem to have been two streams of ethical thinking, one tradition not primarily focused on the law, and another tradition that is a pietistic exposition of the law, often much simplified. Only in a few works such as the *'Iḥyā'* of al-Ghazzālī (d. 505/1111) do the traditions of law and ethics meet.

In Ṣadr's book the argument for man's obligation to God is that a servant has an obligation to a master. This argument is traditional in Shī'ī jurisprudence and represents the thinking of a hierarchical society. In fact, pre-modern Islamic law represents the pre-modern society of Muslims in the Middle East in that it recognizes three different absolute distinctions of status: between male and female, between Muslim and non-Muslim, and between slave and free. This last distinction was discarded as no longer meaningful by Muslim jurists; and the other two distinctions are no longer acceptable. Perhaps Muḥammad Bāqir aṣ-Ṣādr would have written these out of contemporary Islamic law, had he not been savagely killed in his native Iraq on April 8th, 1980 on the order of Saddam Hussein, who subsequently killed scores of Shī'ī jurists to keep his Shī'ī subjects cowed.

Reason and Convention

Earlier in this introduction, I referred to Ṣadr's interest in reason as a source and method in jurisprudence, but in fact we see a mixture of adherence to inherited conventions with a more rationalist approach. In fact, some such mixture is probably present in most legal systems. The adherence to conventionalism is, however, formally much stronger in a system which wishes to refer to scripture on every possible occasion. When Ṣadr tells us that we are looking for "shared or common elements" as the basis for legal reasoning, he is essentially appealing to the authority of the conventions of Islamic jurisprudence, which does not of course exclude the possibility that these conventions might be justified by reason. Sometimes, as in his acceptance of the **single-source account**, he in fact gives only a scriptural justification, since he believes that this source of law is too uncertain to be trusted on a rational basis alone. Since Ṣadr considers the guidance given by reason to be more authoritative than that of a weakly attested hadith, the reader may well ask what the methods of reasoning used are. After all, as we have mentioned above, Ṣadr wrote a book trying to establish the importance – some would say, the primacy – of induction in Shīʿī and, more generally, Islamic legal reasoning. Nevertheless, the relations between all modes of reasoning in determining a rational conclusion have never, to my knowledge, been fully elaborated in Shīʿī jurisprudence.

It can be said in defense of conventionalism that the law reflects the long experience of the society in which it exists. This argument applies more fully to areas such as commercial law than to criminal law, which has been very indifferently enforced in Muslim societies. Moreover, the appeal to the conventions established by great jurists in the past has the virtue of allowing only a limited pluralism when the lack of a formal clerical structure would seem to encourage Islamic law to fly in a thousand directions. In the immediate case of modern Twelver Shīʿīs, the obligation for each believer to follow a living authority, a *mujtahid*, has created a formal structure of religious authority perhaps unparalled in other Muslim communities. The proliferation of Internet fatwas by unqualified jurists stands in strong contrast to this Shīʿī system.

There is another type of conventionalism emphasized by later Shīʿī law which is close to the concept of *ius gentium* in Roman law. Ṣadr, like many of these jurists, speaks of common usage (*ʿurf*) and the **conduct of reasonable people** (*sīra ʿuqalāʾiyya*). These two phrases frequently appear together in Shīʿī works on jurisprudence and substantive law. Common usage and the conduct of reasonable people are subject to change. They are therefore not natural law, which exists for the Shīʿīs because of their belief in God's justice. They are nevertheless some indication as to what natural law might be, and a guide to the way in which laws should be implemented in practice.

A humane aspect of almost all Islamic law is that it takes into consideration the subjective state of the legal agent when assessing accountability. This consideration includes questions of both capacity and **intention**. Shīʿī law of the last two centuries has been especially careful in its discussions of **assurance** in the mind of the legal agent, inspired by, among other things, Avicenna's distinction between **conceptualization** and **assent**. The increased interest in the subjective state of the legal agent is apparent from many passages in this book, and results from two and a half centuries of such discussion in 'Uṣūlī legal circles.

Medieval Western Law and Islamic Law

Earlier I referred to the bishops' courts that existed even before the conversion of the Roman emperors to Christianity. In the fifth Christian century, the Roman emperor Theodosius II sought to define a closed body of authoritative jurists, just as Islamic law did retrospectively with its "authoritative" books of hadith. Similarly, the code prepared under Justinian a century later was subsequently regarded as having a privileged standing as the fullest authoritative statement of Roman law.

The New Testament, notwithstanding the harsh words of Jesus against lawyers and the antinomian tone of some passages in the letters of St. Paul, sometimes praises the law, as when Jesus says, "I tell you the truth, until heaven and earth disappear, not the smallest letter nor the least stroke of the pen will by any means disappear from the Law, until everything is accomplished." (Matthew 5: 18, NIV) It is overwhelmingly likely that Matthew understood Jesus to be speaking of the Jewish law; but as Christianity spread, a more general interpretation became possible. The church grew in an atmosphere pervaded by Roman law, which became more deeply associated with Christianity after the Roman emperor converted in the early fourth century. Yet the west [as contrasted with Byzantium] had to wait until the revival of Roman law in the twelfth century for the church to see the full possibilities that mastery of this sophisticated body of knowledge offered. The greatest figure of this revival, Gratian, who wrote in the first half of the twelfth century, said that the church is both a spiritual and an earthly society. The twelfth century witnessed Western Europe's greatest experiment in religious law. By the thirteenth century, church courts were accepting a great variety of non-ecclesiastical cases. Theologians and canonists were trying to find a firm intellectual connection between the expanding jurisdiction of church-administered Roman law and basic Christian principles.

At some point in the thirteenth century, however, the canonists and the theologians began to part ways. Professor Charles Donahue of the Harvard Law School suggests some contributing reasons for their divergence. First, keeping up with developments in canon law as well as mastering Roman law was a full time occupation, as was the study of theology. Second, as the Church's legal system had to share jurisdiction with secular law, its lawyers had to be able to talk to secular lawyers. The inevitable result was some secularization of canon law. Third, the greatest canonist of the thirteenth century, Henricus de Segusio, and the greatest canonist of the early fourteenth century, the layman Johannes Andreae, seem to have taken no interest in the new scholastic theology and, like other canonists of the period, adhered to the theology of the twelfth century.[8]

Islamic law may have provided for the theoretical possibility of an adoption of pre-Islamic revealed law that would have paralleled the reception of Roman law in Latin Christendom, but in practice Muslim jurists rarely appealed to any previous system. Moreover, the canon lawyers never denied the existence of a secular realm, although they advocated increased Papal oversight of that realm. The *de facto* separation of the authority of sultans from that of the caliph was accepted only as a lesser evil than confrontation and disorder within the Islamic world. Only very rarely was this distinction in the real world defended as an ideal.

Among the Shīʿīs the situation was different. They were seldom in power, and since they had to wait for their messianic leader, they could accept sultans with less theoretical difficulty, demanding primarily that they do justice. Furthermore, their belief in divine justice required them to consider the relation between theology and law a permanently open question. At some periods, their discussion of this relationship was repetitive and unoriginal, at others, innovative. One such innovation is the modern interest in the theoretical basis for extended reliance on common usage and the conduct of reasonable people. And like Aquinas, the ʾUsūlīs could not think of law without scholastic philosophy, whereas many Sunni jurists became great specialists in Islamic law without taking any interest in theology or philosophy or even jurisprudence.

The pre-modern tradition of Islamic learning created a monumental body of scholarship as impressive as that of Europe and India and China. It was successful in creating a sophisticated legal system, which in certain areas, such as commercial law, can be and have been, with some adaptation, successfully applied in the contemporary world. Islamic jurisprudence shared the subtlety of the law it described and remains an intellectual achievement which can be studied with benefit.

The Life of Ṣadr[9]

In 1935 Muḥammad Bāqir aṣ-Ṣadr was born into a family long distinguished in Shīʿī learning and closely associated with Kāẓimayn or Kāẓimiyya, a suburb of Baghdad dominated by the very large and ornate shrine in which two imams of the Twelver Shīʿīs, Mūsā al-Kāẓim (d. 183/799) and his grandson Muḥammad al-Jawād (d. 220/835), are buried. Some report that Ṣadr was allowed to leave home to study at the famous Shīʿī seminary in Najaf as early as his fourteenth year because he was such an unmistakable prodigy. His sister, Amīna Ṣadr (usually called Bint al-Hudā) shared some of her brother's talents and was successful both as a novelist and a public speaker. By 1963 Bāqir aṣ-Ṣadr had begun to teach in Najaf. The leading Shīʿī religious authority at that time in Iraq – and, indeed, in all of the Arab-speaking world – Muḥsin al-Ḥakīm, was antagonistic to the Shīʿī tradition of philosophy. Nevertheless, given Ṣadr's brilliance and reliability, Ḥakīm authorized him to study philosophy with a certain Shaikh Ṣadrā, which would stand him in good stead in his jurisprudence as well as his more purely philosophical work.

It is sometimes forgotten that Iraq was the one Arab country where the local Communist Party once had a real chance of coming to power. Ṣadr and the leading Shīʿī clerics of the time were not only opposed to Communism because of its atheism but also because it had found a fair number of Shīʿī followers. Then as later, the politics of Iraq were dominated by an elite drawn from the Arab Sunni minority and therefore Shīʿīs, including relatives of the most important mullahs, were attracted to the egalitarian promise that Communism seemed to offer. Already in the nineteen-fifties one of the leading thinkers among the Iranian clergy, Muḥammad Ḥusayn Ṭabāṭabāʾi, had written an attack on materialistic philosophies, in particular, Communism, and the very able and prolific Iranian Ayatollah Mortaza Moṭahharī had both popularized and extended this attack. Ṣadr drew on these sources as well as his extensive reading of pro- and anti-Communist literature in Arabic, and on his growing knowledge of Western philosophy as available in Arabic translation, in order to write a series of books that would have enormous readership in the Arab world: *Our Economy*, *Our Philosophy*, *The Interest-Free Bank*, and *The Logical Bases of Induction*, as well as a host of shorter works. All of these books showed his interest in conducting a rigorous discussion in the scholastic style of classical Islamic philosophy as well as in writing a clear and accessible Arabic unlike so many of his predecessors among the Shīʿī clergy. He was limited by the materials available to him and lamented to friends that certain key works had not been translated into Arabic. Whatever future generations may think of them, these works remain a significant part of the history of Arab and Islamic thought in the twentieth century.

Even as Ṣadr labored to combat Communism and to shape a more modern Shīʿī philosophy, he and some like-minded mullahs sought to reform Shīʿī education, both within seminaries and beyond them, much as Moṭahharī had sought to do earlier in Iran. In the sixties, a committee was established to publish textbooks at all levels and there was an attempt to give the seminary at Najaf more structure. Although a new madrasa was founded, attempts to change education in Najaf by and large failed. It has always been a highly individualistic center of learning and less under the control of its leading jurist than Qom, its rival in Iran. A separate attempt to establish a comprehensive university with a Shīʿī orientation at Kufa was quashed by the government. Some of the publications of the period, however, such as Ṣadr's *al-Maʿālim al-Jadīdah* (completed 1965), his first attempt to write an accessible introduction for beginning students of jurisprudence in Najaf, continue to be relevant. Incidentally, the senior clerical figure within the establishment who served as an inspiration for Ṣadr and many lesser jurists was Shaykh Muḥammad Riḍā al-Muẓaffar, whose advanced two-volume work on jurisprudence is still considered standard.

In the background of the political life of Iraqi Shīʿīs from the time of the Iraqi revolution of 1958 was the clandestine political party called the Daʿwa. Ṣadr certainly knew about the party from the beginning and some claim he was the founder and its moving spirit. The secularist governments in Baghdad were also aware of the party's existence and, while denying it any legality, used its members in the balancing act with which the regime would alternately set the Communists, the Baathists, the religious Shīʿīs and other factions against each other. The Daʿwa wished to create an "Islamic" Iraq although the concrete content of "Islamicness" was differently understood by different members of the party. It had some Sunni members. But the Shīʿī Arabs, some sixty percent of the population, although divided into several parties, saw the Daʿwa as the most direct claimant for the right of religious Shīʿīs to organize politically. Ayatollah Muḥsin al-Ḥakīm, the most authoritative clergyman in Najaf, was very much against political activism and rumor has it that in 1961 he ordered Ṣadr to sever his ties with the Daʿwa. For most of the sixties the Shīʿī clergy and the government dealt with each other at arm's length. There was an understanding that except in extraordinary circumstances no clergyman protected by al-Ḥakīm would be arrested.

When Ayatollah Ḥakīm died in 1970 the great majority of Iraqi Shīʿī clerics recognized the distinguished jurist Abu l-Qāsim al-Khūʾī, as his successor. Ṣadr was in the forefront of those recognizing Khūʾī who had been his teacher, and whose views on jurisprudence continued to influence him. Nevertheless, at about the same time Ṣadr issued a manual of guidance for the lay Shīʿī believer that more or less put forward the claim that Ṣadr had the standing to succeed Khūʾī. This claim was widely accepted. Khūʾī wished to avoid confrontation and in general Ṣadr followed his lead, although after the return of the Baathists to power in July 1968 the government began to arrest clergymen and Ṣadr sometimes spoke out on their behalf.

In 1977 the relations between the Shīʿī clergy and the government broke down. The Baathists, determined to show who was in control, banned the annual procession from Najaf to Karbala that commemorates the martyrdom of Ḥusayn, which is for Shīʿīs the most deeply tragic event in their history. Nevertheless, some tens of thousands of Shīʿīs followed the procession. When the marchers arrived in Karbala, the Iraqi security forces imprisoned several hundred of them. The Baathist regime, still split after many years, could not agree how to manage the incident. The faction dominated by Saddam Hussein gained control and decided that any kind of Shīʿī challenge must have been masterminded by Ṣadr. He was arrested, but the Baathist government was not yet willing to deal with the level of anger that this arrest caused among the Shīʿīs and he was released.

The Iranian revolution in 1978 sharply increased the tension created in the preceding year. The details of Ṣadr's relations with the Daʿwa party still remain something of a mystery, but there is no question that the party was vastly emboldened by events in Iran and looked to Ṣadr for leadership. Everything seemed possible when the Shah, America's "policeman of the Gulf" and the "heir of two and a half millennia of kingship," simply packed and left. Some say that Ṣadr tried to restrain the Daʿwa, assuring them that eventually their time would come. Nevertheless, Ṣadr had become more politically active himself. Some claim that he told his classes that a good Shīʿī could not belong to the Baath party. Demonstrations held openly in the name of the Daʿwa party occurred in Shīʿī towns. The government arrested Ṣadr along with hundreds of others. Riots broke out and Ṣadr was released, only to be put under house arrest. His interrogator in August 1979 allegedly offered to release him if he made any one of several proposed major public concessions to the government. Ṣadr at this point seems to have chosen martyrdom and refused any cooperation with the government. Attacks on the government by the Daʿwa increased. On April 5, 1980 the government arrested him and his sister, who had given impassioned sermons in protest at his earlier arrest. They were executed on April 8th. In the following September Iraq began its eight year war against Iran, as Saddam Hussein had decided that political Shīʿism was his greatest enemy and had by now killed many clergymen and hundreds of followers of the Daʿwa party. The million casualties incurred in the Iran-Iraq war were, given the size of the two countries involved, comparable to casualties in Europe in the First and Second World Wars. Iranians continue to believe that Iraq was given a green light to start the war (as well as being bolstered during the war) by the United States, which then shared the Baathist view that Ṣadr was Iraq's Khomeini.

Ṣadr's intellectual activities in the seventies are still disputed. Later historians have tried to make Ṣadr and Khomeini part of the same story, but in fact they had somewhat different orientations. Muhsin al-Hakim was the leader of Iraqi Shīʿīs when Khomeini settled in Najaf. Khūʾī's circle regarded Khomeini as too political and too reckless in the expression of his political views. Ṣadr certainly shared Khomeini's desire for "Islamic government", but it is overwhelmingly likely that Ṣadr followed his teacher Khūʾī in disapproving of Khomeini's theory of the "guardianship of the jurist." Clergymen in Najaf remember Ṣadr and Khomeini as having cordial, but not particularly close, relations. All changed with the approach of the Iranian revolution. Ṣadr wrote in favor of the "guardianship of the jurist" and told his followers that they should "melt" into Khomeini's movement.

Yet during the seventies, in the midst of this turmoil and change, he wrote his *Lessons in Islamic Jurisprudence*, which shows him to be – in his field of greatest competence – not a follower but very much his own man. The first volume, translated here, is meant for students of approximately eighteen years of age; it has become part of the curriculum of several madrasas, and itself the subject of commentaries. It is followed by two more volumes, and I very much regret that I have not found the time to translate the second volume of the series, which clarifies many issues left hanging in the first.

Had Ṣadr lived, he would have continued to revise his views as he did throughout his life. I do not believe he would have sought political union with Iran, despite the religious sympathies the two nations shared. Ṣadr was thoroughly Iraqi and Arab. He understood Persian well but never tried to speak it. Ṣadr so admired the zeal and style of the Egyptian Sunni writer Sayyid Quṭb that he had Muḥsin al-Ḥakīm send a telegram to President Nasser on the occasion of

Quṭb's death. Ṣadr's cousin used to demand that no classes be taught in Persian in Najaf even though so many of the students came from Iran. When, with American encouragement, the Iraqi Shīʿīs rose against the government in 1991, it was portraits of Ṣadr that were displayed everywhere. At the present the fate of Iraq is uncertain, but there is no way it can be resolved without accepting the strong self-consciousness of the Iraqi Shīʿī community that Ṣadr did so much to shape.

Notes

1. See pp. 4–5 of Wael B. Hallaq, *A History of Islamic Legal Theories*, Cambridge: CUP, 1999, one of the most serious and helpful introductions to Sunni jurisprudence. My introduction leans heavily on the scholarship of others. I do not attempt to cite sources for information well known among specialists in Islamic jurisprudence.
2. N.J. Coulson and R. Le Tourneau, "Bayt al-Māl," *Encyclopaedia of Islam*, 2nd edn, Leiden: E.J. Brill, 1960, I: 114b.
3. J. Schacht, "Ibn 'Abī Laylā," *Encyclopaedia of Islam*, 2nd edn, Leiden: E.J. Brill, 1971, III: 687.
4. See Roy P. Mottahedeh, "Towards an Islamic Theology of Toleration," *Islamic Law Reform and Human Rights*, eds T. Lindholm and K. Vogt, Oslo, 1992, pp. 25–36.
5. Eric Chaumont, "Shāfiʿī," *Encyclopaedia of Islam*, 2nd edn, Leiden: E.J. Brill, 1995, IX: 181–4.
6. Ibn aṣ-Ṣalāh, *Muqaddimah Ibn aṣ-Ṣalāh*, Cairo: Dār al-Maʿārif, 1411/1990, pp. 453–5. I am grateful to Dr. Aron Zysow for this reference.
7. Hossein Modarressi-Tabataba'i, *An Introduction to Shiʿi Law: A Bibliographical Study*, London: Ithaca Press, 1984, p. 4 and note 2, in which Muḥammad Bāqir aṣ-Ṣadr is quoted as saying that reason is a potential rather than actual source of law.

8. Charles Donahue, "A Crisis of Law? Reflections on the Church and the Law over the Centuries," forthcoming.
9. This introduction does not include a biography or more general treatment of the intellectual contribution of Muḥammad Bāqir aṣ-Ṣādr. On these subjects see the outstanding book by Chibli Mallat, *The Renewal of Islamic Law: Muhammad Baqer as-Sadr, Najaf and the Shi'i International*, Cambridge: CUP, 1993.

1

Characterization of Jurisprudence

A Preliminary Word

As a human being who has believed in God, Islam and the **Divine law** and has recognized a responsibility, by virtue of being a servant to God Most High, to follow His **rulings**, one becomes obligated to conform one's behavior in the various fields of life to the Islamic divine law and obligated to adopt a **practical position** which adherence to the divine law imposes. For this reason it is a human being's duty to determine this practical position and to know how to behave in every eventuality.

Had the rulings of the divine law for all events been totally and **self-evidently** clear to all, then to define the desirable practical position vis-à-vis the divine law would be an easy matter for everyone, and would not require learned investigation and extensive study. But numerous factors, such as our distance in time from the age of legislation, have lead to the lack of clarity of a large number of rulings of the divine law and to their being surrounded by obscurity. Thus it was necessary that a discipline be established that would undertake to remove obscurity concerning the practical position before the divine law in every eventuality by establishing an **argument** for determining the [practical] position.

Thus the discipline of **legal understanding** was founded to undertake this task. It includes determining by inference the practical position vis-à-vis the divine law. The **jurist** [*i.e.*, the specialist in the discipline of legal understanding] undertakes to establish an argument which attempts to specify the practical position in every one of the events of life. This is what we have designated "the procedure of **derivation** of a divine-law ruling." For this reason one can say that the discipline of legal understanding is the discipline of the derivation of rulings of the divine law, or, in other words, the discipline of the procedure of such derivation.

To determine the practical position before the divine law through an argument is accomplished in the discipline of legal understanding in two ways. The first way is to determine the practical position by identifying an appropriate divine-law ruling. The second way, which applies when one is quite sure that one can only doubtfully identify the appropriate ruling, is to identify the appropriate duty in practice. The arguments which are used in the first case we call merely "arguments" or **substantiating arguments**, since the divine-law ruling is substantiated by them. The arguments which are used in the second case are called "procedural arguments" or **procedural principles**. In both cases the jurist practices the derivation of a divine-law ruling, that is, he determines the practical position in the case at hand with an argument.

The procedures of derivation which the discipline of legal understanding includes, in spite of their number and variety, share common unifying elements and common rules which pertain to all of them. It is these shared elements in the procedure of derivation that required the establishment of a new discipline which specializes in studying them and defining them and adapting them to the existing discipline of legal understanding; and so the discipline of **jurisprudence** came into existence.

Characterization of Jurisprudence

On this basis we consider it correct to define the discipline of jurisprudence as "knowledge of the shared elements in the procedure of derivation of the divine law." In order that we comprehend this definition it is necessary for us to characterize the shared elements in the procedure of derivation. Let us mention for this purpose elementary examples of this procedure in brief in order that by study and comparison we may arrive at a definite idea of what the common elements in the procedure of derivation are.

Suppose that the jurist (the specialist in the divine law) faces these questions:

1. When fasting, is it forbidden to immerse oneself in water?
2. Is it obligatory for someone who inherits property from his father to pay the tax of one-**fifth** on it?
3. Is prayer nullified by laughing out loud in the course of it?

(1) When the jurist wishes to answer these questions, he will for example answer the first question in the affirmative, saying that immersion in water is forbidden to one who fasts. He derives this answer as follows: the account of Ya'qūb b. Shu'ayb transmitted from **Imam** Ja'far aṣ-Ṣādiq has indicated the prohibitedness for the fasting person of immersion in water, since from that account we learn that [Ja'far] said: "Neither the one in a state of ritual consecration required of the pilgrim nor the person fasting should immerse himself in water." This sentence, given its particular construction, indicates prohibitedness according to **common usage**. The transmitter of the **account** is a reliable transmitter, and the **Lawgiver** has commanded us not to suspect a reliable transmitter of error or lying. Although he may at times make a mistake or relate idiosyncratic accounts, yet we are to consider him as a source of **evidence**. The conclusion is that immersion in water is prohibited.

(2) The jurist answers the second question in the negative because there has come down to us an account from ʿAlī b. Mahziyār about the issue of exactly how to determine on what property the one-fifth tax is payable. It emerges from that account that paying the fifth is firmly established only as regards an unexpected inheritance, *sc.* in a case that involves neither the son inheriting after the death of the father, nor the father after the death of the son. The common-usage understanding of such a formulation is that the Lawgiver did not impose the one-fifth tax upon a father–son transfer. The transmitter of the account is a reliable source and what comes from a reliable source is evidence. The conclusion is that the son does not owe the fifth on what his father leaves him.
(3) The jurist answers the third question in the affirmative with the [substantiating] argument of an account from Zurāra citing Imam Jaʿfar aṣ-Ṣādiq as saying "Laughing out loud does not destroy the validity of ablution, but it does destroy the validity of prayer." Common usage understands from "destroying the validity" that prayer is nullified by laughter out loud. Zurāra is a reliable transmitter and the account of a reliable transmitter is evidence. Accordingly, prayer accompanied by laughter out loud is nullified.

In considering these three legal-understanding cases we find that the rulings which the jurist has derived are about entirely unrelated topics of legal understanding. The arguments upon which the jurist relies are varied. We observe that the first ruling relied on the account of Yaʿqūb b. Shuʿayb, while the second ruling relied upon the account of ʿAlī b. Mahziyār, and the third ruling upon the account of Zurāra. Each of the three accounts has its own exact text and its own exact linguistic construction, which require to be studied with care and the meaning thereof determined. Yet despite all this variety and difference between the three cases, there exist common elements which the jurist has introduced into his derivation in all three cases alike. Among these common elements is the recourse to common usage for understanding speech emanating from an **infallible person**. That is what is called **probativity** of the **prima-facie** understanding of common usage. Thus "probativity of the prima-facie understanding" is one element shared by all three of these procedures of derivation. Similarly, another shared element which exists here is "the probativity of the reliable source."

Thus we conclude that the procedures of derivation include general elements as well as particular elements. By "particular elements" we mean those elements which change from one question to the next. The account of Ya'qūb b. Shu'ayb, [for instance,] is an element particular [in its significance] for the procedure of the derivation of the forbidden nature of immersion in water, because it has not entered into other procedures of derivation. Rather, in its place other particular elements such as the account of 'Alī b. Mahziyār and the account of Zurārah have been introduced.

By "general elements" we mean the rules which are introduced into procedures of derivation of numerous rulings on various topics. Such shared elements are studied by jurisprudence, whereas the elements particular to each individual question are studied by the discipline of legal understanding.

In this way in each question it is left to the jurist carefully to investigate the particular accounts and sources that are connected with that question. He studies the value of these accounts and tries to understand the **utterances** in them and their common-usage prima-facie sense and the chains along which they have been transmitted. The specialist in jurisprudence, however, takes up the discussion of the probativity of the prima-facie sense, the probativity of transmitted reports, and so on. The discipline of jurisprudence does not just define the common elements, it also defines both the degrees to which they should be used and the connection between them, as – God Most High willing – we shall see in our coming discussions.

The Subject-Matter of Jurisprudence

Normally, every discipline has a basic subject-matter around which all of its discussions revolve and on which all are based, and you have as your goal to uncover the particularities, conditions and laws that are connected with that subject. Physics, for example, takes nature as its subject-matter and discussions in physics are all connected with nature and attempt to uncover its phenomena and common laws. The subject-matter of grammar is the word because grammar discusses the conditions of its case inflections, the indeclinability of the word, and its declinability with different suffixes. Then what is the subject-matter of jurisprudence around which its discussions revolve?

When we consider the definition of the discipline of jurisprudence which we have put forward, we can grasp that jurisprudence in reality studies the commonly shared arguments [used] in the discipline of legal understanding in order to establish their force as arguments. It is, therefore, correct to say that the subject-matter of the discipline of jurisprudence is the commonly shared arguments in the process of derivation.

The Discipline of Jurisprudence is the Logic of Legal Understanding

Your knowledge of the discipline of logic permits us to use it as an example for the discipline of jurisprudence, since, as you know, the science of logic in reality studies the process of thinking whatever its intellectual scope and field may be. Logic defines the general structure that must be followed in order that thinking be sound. For example, the discipline of logic teaches us how we must proceed by **inference** in its quality as a procedure of thought in order that the inference be correct. How do we infer that Socrates is a mortal? How do we infer that the fire of the stove placed in front of us is burning? How do we infer that the sum of the angles of a triangle equals one hundred and eighty degrees? How do we infer that a line extended without **limit** is impossible? The discipline of logic answers all this by establishing general methods of inference like deduction and induction. It is, therefore, a discipline concerned simply with the process of thought as such.

In this respect the discipline of jurisprudence resembles the discipline of logic except that it discusses a particular variety of thought process, that is, the legal-understanding thought process concerning the derivation of rulings. It studies the shared elements that must be introduced into the process in order that the derivation be sound. So it instructs us about how we derive the ruling of the forbidden nature of immersion for someone who fasts, how we derive the impossibility of water above a certain quantity becoming impure, and how we derive the ruling that the liturgical prayer on the Feast of Sacrifice is either obligatory or encouraged. It does so by laying down the shared methods and by defining the common elements for the process of derivation.

On this basis it is correct to call the discipline of jurisprudence "the logic of the discipline of legal understanding," because jurisprudence stands to the discipline of legal understanding just as logic stands to human thought in general.

The Importance of the Discipline of Jurisprudence in the Practice of Derivation

After this we have no need to emphasize the importance of the science of jurisprudence and the significance of its role in the sphere of derivation because, inasmuch as jurisprudence provides the shared elements for the process of derivation and establishes their general structure, it is the life vein [of derivation]. Without the science of jurisprudence a person would face a scattered heap of texts and arguments without being able to use them and benefit from them in the effort to derive a ruling, like a man who stands before tools of carpentry and is given a saw and an ax and similar tools without possessing general ideas of the procedure of carpentry and the method of using these tools. Just as shared elements are necessary for the process of derivation, similarly there are particular elements which differ from one question to the next such as the individual scriptural verses and the scattered accounts relevant to the question, for they constitute the other part necessary in this process. Therefore, mere knowledge of the shared elements that are described by the science of jurisprudence is not enough. Anyone who tries to perform derivation on the basis of jurisprudential knowledge alone is like one who possesses general theoretical information about the process of carpentry but has no ax or saw or similar carpentry tool. Just as such a person would, for example, be incapable of making a wooden bed, similarly the expert in jurisprudence would be incapable of derivation if he/she did not carefully scrutinize the particular elements that vary from one case to the next. Thus the shared and particular elements are the two poles incorporated in the process of derivation, and both alike are indispensable for the process.

Jurisprudence is to Legal Understanding as Theory is to Application

We fear we may have inspired a mistaken conception in you when we explained that in the discipline of jurisprudence one who derives [rulings] studies shared elements and defines them, whereas in discussions of the discipline of legal understanding such a person avails himself of particular elements in order to complete the process of derivation. Some may suppose that when in jurisprudence we have studied the shared elements in the process of derivation and have, for example, recognized the probativity of the account related and the probativity of the prima-facie meaning and additional jurisprudential elements, no further intellectual effort is incumbent upon us, since, seeing that we have mastered these elements, we need the mere extraction of relevant accounts and **prooftexts** from their places in the sources in order for them to be added to the shared elements and for the divine-law ruling to be derived from them, and that this is an easy task by its nature which does not involve any intellectual effort.

Yet this conception is erroneous to a great degree because the **jurisconsult**, when s/he employs the shared elements for the process of derivation and defines them for the science of jurisprudence, is not content after that to gather blindly the elements particular to the case from the books of **traditions** and accounts. Rather, his/her obligation in the discipline of legal understanding remains the application of those shared elements and general theories to the particular elements, and the application is an intellectual task which, by its nature, requires study and close examination. The intellectual effort expended as a specialist in jurisprudence does not free one from expending a further effort in the application [of jurisprudential principles]. Let us suppose, for example, that in the discipline of jurisprudence the specialist in jurisprudence is convinced of the probativity of the prima-facie meaning as commonly understood. Is it, then, sufficient for him/her to point to the account of ʿAlī b. Mahziyār which defines the items subject to the one-fifth tax, for example, so that he may add that account to the shared element and thereby derive the ruling that an inheritance from one's father is not taxable since it is not mentioned among the items subject to the one-fifth tax? Does the jurisconsult not need precisely to determine what is signified by the prooftext in the account in order to understand the category of the thing signified according to common usage, and to study everything connected with determining the prima-facie meaning in common usage from **contexts** and **indications** internal or external to the prooftext, in order to be able confidently to apply the shared element which proposes the probativity of the prima-facie meaning in common usage? In this light we understand that legal discussion concerning the particular elements in the process of derivation is not merely an act of gathering, but is the domain of the application of jurisprudential theories. The application of general jurisprudential theories requires its own particular talent and meticulousness. Being meticulous merely about general jurisprudential theories does not free one from the need to be meticulous about their application. How evident it is that one who studies general theories of medicine in depth must, in the domain of their application to a case of illness, exercise meticulousness, total attentiveness and reflectiveness in applying these theories to the patient before him!

The Interaction Between Legal-Understanding Thought and Jurisprudential Thought

We have recognized that the discipline of jurisprudence plays the role of logic in respect to the discipline of legal understanding and that the relation between the two is the relation between theory and application. This close interconnectedness between the two explains to us the mutual interaction between the jurisprudential cast of mind on the level of theories on the one hand, and the legal-understanding cast of mind on the level of application on the other, because the expansion of discussions of application impels discussion of theory a step forward. It does so because it stirs up difficulties as it advances and necessitates the establishment of general theories for their solution. Similarly, meticulousness of inquiry into jurisprudential theories is reflected at the level of application since, insofar as the theories become more comprehensive and more precise, the method of their application demands greater precision and depth. This interaction between the two casts of mind, that of jurisprudence and that of legal understanding, is confirmed throughout the history of the two disciplines. A study of the stages which legal-understanding and jurisprudential inquiry have passed through in the history of the disciplines reveals this with great clarity, for the discipline of jurisprudence developed in the midst of the discipline of legal understanding just as legal understanding developed in the midst of the discipline of tradition.

At first, the discipline of jurisprudence was not independent of the discipline of legal understanding. As the discipline of legal understanding grew and the horizons of legal thinking expanded, common threads and shared elements in the process of derivation began to appear and come to light. The practitioners of legal understanding began to observe the participation of these procedures in common elements without which a divine-law ruling could not be derived. This development was a sign of the birth of the discipline of jurisprudence and the adoption by the legal-understanding cast of mind of a jurisprudential orientation. So the discipline of jurisprudence separated from the discipline of legal understanding at the level both of discussion and of writing. It began to broaden and flourish gradually through the growth of jurisprudential thought on the one hand, and due to the expansion of legal inquiry on the other hand, because the expansion of the scope of the application of the law continually directed the attention of practitioners to new difficulties, and appropriate solutions for them were being proposed. These solutions were beginning to take the form of shared elements in the discipline of jurisprudence.

To the degree that the jurist became distant from the age of prooftexts, the aspects of obscurity in derivation from its divine-law sources became more numerous, and as a result of the distance in time, the gaps in the process of derivation became more diverse. And so the need was more and more keenly felt to define some general principles by which to treat these aspects of obscurity and to fill these gaps. In this way the need for the discipline of jurisprudence was a historical matter, in the sense that the need became stronger and more unmistakable the farther the specialists in law became distant historically from the age of the prooftexts, and the more doubts accumulated about the process of derivation that they practiced.

On this basis we can explain the disparity in time between the flourishing of the discipline of jurisprudence in the domain of Sunni legal thought and its flourishing in the domain of Twelver Shīʿī legal thought, for history indicates that the discipline of jurisprudence matured and flourished earlier in the domain of Sunni law than it matured and flourished in our Twelver Shīʿī legal domain. That earlier flourishing occurred because the Sunni school maintained that the age of prooftexts ended with the death of the Prophet. So when Sunni legal thought entered the second Islamic century it had already become distant from the age of prooftexts by a long period of time, a situation which by its nature created breaches and gaps [in legal understanding].

As for the Twelver Shīʿīs, at that point they were still living in the age of prooftexts because the Imam is an extension of the existence of the Prophet. So the problems that concerned the Twelver Shīʿī jurists in derivation were a great deal less troubling, so much so that there was no room to feel a strong need to establish a discipline of jurisprudence. For this reason we find that in Twelver Shīʿism, by the mere fact that the age of divinely inspired provision ended for them with the beginning of the Occultation [260/874] or, more particularly, the end of the Lesser Occultation [329/940], the jurisprudential cast of mind only started among them at that time and they embarked upon the study of shared elements. Naturally, this does not mean that the seeds of jurisprudential thought did not exist among the jurists who were companions of the Imams. Rather these seeds had existed from the times of the Imams Muḥammad al-Bāqir and Jaʿfar aṣ-Ṣādiq on a level appropriate for that stage of development. Among the historical evidence for that are those things transmitted in the books of tradition, questions related to a number of shared elements in the process of derivation. A number of transmitters [of traditions] directed such questions to Imam Jaʿfar aṣ-Ṣādiq and other Imams and received answers from them. These questions reveal the existence of the seed of jurisprudential thinking among them. Some of the companions of the Imams wrote treatises on certain jurisprudential questions, such as Hishām b. al-Ḥakam among the companions of Imam [Jaʿfar] aṣ-Ṣādiq, about whom [sc. Hishām] it is related that he wrote a treatise on utterances, which strengthens the case [that the seeds of jurisprudential thinking existed among the Shīʿīs in that early period].

The Permissibility of the Process of Deriving Divine-Legal Rulings

As long as the discipline of jurisprudence remains bound up with the process of derivation and defines the shared elements in that process, it is necessary that, before anything else, we know the position of the divine law in regard to this process: Does the Lawgiver permit anyone to exercise this process so that scope be created to establish a discipline for the study of the shared elements?

The truth is that the question of the permissibility of derivation, when it is put forward for discussion in the form in which we have put it forward, does not appear to be worthy of debate. For when we ask ourselves whether we are permitted to undertake the procedure of derivation, then the answer that comes spontaneously is positive. It is positive because, as has been said above, the process of derivation consists of defining the practical position before the divine law by the use of inference. It is self-evident that a human by virtue of adherence to the divine law is obligated to define his/her practical position before it. When the rulings of the divine law are not overwhelmingly self-evident and clear to a degree which relieves one of any need to establish an argument, then it is not logical that people be forbidden to define their practical position through inference.

Unfortunately, however, this question happens to have acquired another form not lacking some degree of obscurity and confusion. This form of the question has become the cause of disagreement among the jurists on account of this obscurity and confusion. This situation exists because the word **ijtihad** has been used to express the idea of a process of derivation. In this way the question has been asked: Is *ijtihad* permissible in the divine law? When the word *ijtihad* enters the question – and it is a word which has passed through numerous technical meanings in its history – it results in the shadow of those previous technical meanings being cast upon the discussion. As a result, some have answered the question negatively. This in turn led to the condemnation of the entire discipline of jurisprudence because it was desired only for the sake of *ijtihad*. If *ijtihad* was declared invalid, there was not considered to be any need for the discipline of jurisprudence.

In the course of clarifying this it is necessary that we mention the development through which the word *ijtihad* passed in order to clarify how the dispute which occurred over the permissibility of the process of derivation and the outcry that was aroused against it were the result only of an inexact understanding of the technical vocabulary and of inattention to the transformations through which the word *ijtihad* passed in the history of the discipline.

Ijtihad is lexically derived from *jahd*, which means "expending one's utmost effort to carry out some task." This word had first been used in the legal sphere to express one of the principles which some Sunni legal schools laid down and proceeded with, namely, that the jurist, when he wants to derive a legal ruling and does not find a specific divine **injunction** indicating the [relevant] ruling in the Qur'ān or sunna, has recourse to *ijtihad* in place of specific divine injunction. Here *ijtihad* means personal thinking: the jurist when s/he does not find a prooftext has recourse to his/her particular thinking, seeks inspiration from it and builds on the basis of making the law be whatever seems preferable according to his/her personal thought. This is sometimes also called **opinion**.

Ijtihad in this sense is considered one of the arguments used by the jurist and one of his/her sources. Just as the jurist may rely on Qur'ān and sunna and make inferences on the basis of both alike, similarly in situations of the unavailability of a prooftext s/he relies on personal *ijtihad* and makes legal inferences on the basis of it.

Major schools in Sunni law proclaimed this idea, the leader among them being the school of 'Abū Ḥanīfa. At the same time this idea encountered strenuous opposition from the Imams of the Family of the Prophet [recognized by the Twelver Shī'īs] and the jurists who adhered to their school.

Tracing the word *ijtihad* indicates that the word carried this meaning and was used to express it from the time of the Imams until the seventh Islamic [13th C.E.] century. The accounts transmitted from the Shī'ī Imams condemn *ijtihad*, meaning by it that legal principle which adopts personal thinking as one of the sources of a ruling. The attack on this legal principle had also entered the realm of writing in the age of the Imams and in the age of the transmitters who conveyed what the Imams left behind. The attack usually made use of the word *ijtihad* to express that principle in a way that agrees with the technical use which occurs elsewhere in the accounts of the Imams. 'Abd Allāh b. 'Abd ar-Raḥmān az-Zubayr [*floruit c.* 250/870] wrote a book entitled *The Benefit: Concerning the Attacks on the first Caliphs and a Rejection of the Users of* Ijtihad *and* Analogy. Hilāl b. Ibrahīm b. 'Abī l-Fatḥ al-Madanī wrote a book on the subject entitled *A Refutation of Those who Reject the Reports of the Prophet and Rely on the Results of Intellects*. In the period of the Lesser Occultation [260/874 – 329/941] or near to that time, 'Isma'īl b. 'Alī b. 'Isḥāq b. 'Abī Sahl an-Nawbakhtī [died 311/923] wrote a book refuting 'Isā b. 'Abān on *ijtihad*. All of this is set down by an-Najāshī [died 450/1058], the author of *Ar-Rijāl*, in his biographical notices of each of the above.

In the period succeeding the Lesser Occultation we find [Ibn Babawayh al-Qumī] aṣ-Ṣaddūq in the mid-fourth [eleventh] century continuing this attack. As an example we mention his comment on the story of Moses and al-Khiḍr, when he wrote:

> Moses, in spite of the perfection of his intellect and his excellence and his position [as a prophet] in relation to God Most High, failed to comprehend the meaning of the actions of al-Khiḍr with his powers of inference and deriving conclusions, so much so that Moses became confused as to the nature of the situation. If **analogy** and derivation and inference are not permissible for the Prophets of God and His Messengers, then how much more so must those below them among the religious communities not be permitted them! If the option to choose [an interpretation] was not correct for Moses, in spite of his excellence and his position, then how can a religious community be fit to have the option of choosing the Imam, and how are they fit to derive divine-law rulings and infer them with their imperfect intellects and differing opinions?

In the latter part of the fourth century Shaykh al-Mufīd [died 413/1022] came and followed the same line and attacked *ijtihad*, referring by this word to the above-mentioned legal principle [of private judgment]. He wrote a book on this subject entitled *A Refutation of 'Alī b. al-Junayd [al-'Iskāfī] Concerning the* Ijtihad *of Individual Opinion*.

We find the term itself in the works of as-Sayyid al-Murtaḍā [died 436/1034] in the early part of the fifth century, when he wrote in *adh-Dharīʿa* condemning *ijtihad*, saying "*Ijtihad* is invalid, and the **Imamiyya** do not consider it permissible to proceed according to supposition or individual opinion or *ijtihad*." In his legal book *al-Intiṣār* he wrote, referring to Ibn al-Junayd, "It is a kind of individual opinion and *ijtihad* that Ibn al-Junayd relied upon in this question and his error is evident." And on the question of wiping the top of both feet clean in ablution, he says in the chapter on **purity** of *al-Intiṣār*, "We do not consider *ijtihad* correct and do not advocate it."

This particular use of the word *ijtihad* also continued after that time. Thus ash-Shaykh aṭ-Ṭūsī who died in the middle of the fifth century A.H. writes in his book *al-ʿUdda*, "As for analogy and *ijtihad*, in our school they are not arguments; rather, their use is prohibited." In the latter part of the sixth century Ibn 'Idrīs [died 598/1202] in his book *aṣ-Ṣarāʾir* in his discussion of the question of the contradiction of two oral testimonies reviews a number of the reasons for preferring one testimony over another, then comments "According to the followers of our school there is no other reason for giving preference [to one testimony over another]; analogy, **discretionary opinion** and *ijtihad* are invalid in our school."

These texts in their continuous historical sequence indicate that the word *ijtihad* was an expression of that legal principle down to the beginning of the seventh century A.H. On this basis the word acquired an odious coloration and a character of despicability and loathsomeness in the Twelver Shīʿī legal mind as a result of the opposition to that principle and faith in its invalidity.

Yet the word *ijtihad* underwent developments thereafter in the technical vocabulary of our jurists. We do not at present have a Shīʿī text reflecting that development historically earlier than *Kitāb al-Maʿārij* by al-Muḥaqqiq al-Ḥillī (who died in 676 A.H. [1277 C.E.]) when under the heading "The True Nature of Ijtihād" al-Muḥaqqiq wrote:

> [*Ijtihad*] in the common usage of the jurists is the expending one's utmost effort to extract legal rulings. In this sense extracting legal

> rulings from the arguments of the law is a kind of *ijtihad*, because these rulings are constructed on theoretical considerations which have in most part not been derived from the prima-facie meanings of the prooftexts, whether the argument [for these rulings] be analogy or something else. So, according to this account, analogy is a kind of *ijtihad*. If it is said – on this basis – that the Imamiyya must be among the partisans of *ijtihad*, we agree that such is the case. Yet there is something confusing about it since analogy is part of *ijtihad*. Setting aside analogy, however, we are among the partisans of *ijtihad* in obtaining rulings by theoretical means, of which analogy is not one.

On the basis of this text it is clearly observable that the word *ijtihad* continued to be burdened in the basic mental outlook of jurists with the consequence of its first technical use. This is why al-Ḥillī's text alludes to the existence of those who hold themselves aloof from this description and for whom it is difficult to describe the jurists of the Twelver Shīʿīs as practitioners of *ijtihad*.

However, al-Muḥaqqiq al-Ḥillī himself did not stand aloof from the word *ijtihad* after he developed its meaning – or it evolved in the common usage of jurists – in a way that would allow it to agree with the methods of legal derivation used in Twelver Shīʿī legal understanding, since, while *ijtihad* was a source for the jurist on which s/he drew and an argument with which s/he made inferences just as s/he draws on a Qur'ānic verse or a tradition, *ijtihad* came in its new technical meaning to express the effort [*jahd*, as above] which the jurist expends in extracting a divine-law ruling from its arguments and sources. Thus [*ijtihad*] was not considered one of the sources of derivation, but rather the process which the jurist practices of deriving a ruling from its sources.

The difference between the two meanings is essential in the utmost degree, since, according to the first technical use of *ijtihad*, it was the jurist's obligation to derive rulings from his personal thinking and his particular inclination in a case in which no prooftext is available. If the jurist is asked "What is your argument and the source of this ruling of yours?," he will offer *ijtihad* as the basis on which he drew conclusions and say "The argument is my *ijtihad* and my particular thinking." But the new technical meaning does not permit the jurist to bring forward any ruling on the basis of *ijtihad*, because *ijtihad* in the second sense is not a source of the ruling but rather the process of derivation of rulings from their sources. If the jurist should say "This is my *ijtihad*," his meaning would be "This is what I have derived from the sources and arguments." And then we would have the right to ask questions and demand that he indicate to us those sources and arguments from which he derived the ruling.

This new meaning for the word *ijtihad* also passed through a certain amount of development. Al-Muḥaqqiq al-Ḥillī had confined it to the area of processes of derivation that do not rely on the prima-facie meanings of prooftexts. So any process of legal derivation that does not rely on the prima-facie senses of prooftexts is called *ijtihad*, to the exclusion of what does depend on such prima-facie meanings. Perhaps the impulse to this confinement of the meaning [of *ijtihad*] is that the derivation of a ruling from the prima-facie sense of a prooftext does not involve such a great deal of effort [*jahd* again] or intellectual strain that it should be called [any sort of] *ijtihad*.

Then the scope of *ijtihad* subsequently widened. It came to include the process of derivation from the prima-facie sense of a prooftext as well, because the specialists in jurisprudence subsequently observed correctly that the process of derivation from the prima-facie sense of a prooftext absorbs a great deal of intellectual effort as one proceeds to gain knowledge of that prima-facie sense and determine what it is and establish the probativity of the prima-facie sense in common usage. The extension of the meaning of *ijtihad* as a technical term did not stop at this limit. Rather, in a new development it came to include all aspects of the process of derivation. Every process which the jurist practices to determine one's practical position before the divine law, whether by way of establishing an argument for the divine-law ruling or by directly specifying the practical position, enters into the realm of *ijtihad*.

In this way *ijtihad* became synonymous with the process of derivation. Subsequently the discipline of jurisprudence became the discipline necessary for *ijtihad* because it is knowledge of the shared elements in the process of derivation.

In this light we can explain the position of a group of our outstanding scholars who opposed the word *ijtihad* because of the heritage it bore from its first technical use against which [the Imams,] the people of the House [of the Prophet,] launched a severe attack. It differs from *ijtihad* in the second meaning. Seeing that we have now distinguished between the two meanings of *ijtihad*, we can restore to the matter its self-evidential nature and see with great clarity the permissibility of *ijtihad* in the meaning synonymous with the procedure of derivation, and from that follows the necessity of preserving the discipline of jurisprudence in order to study the shared elements in the process of derivation.

2

Substantiating Arguments

The Divine-Law Ruling and its Subdivision

We have understood that the discipline of jurisprudence studies the shared elements in the process of derivation. On this account it is necessary that there be a general idea from the start concerning the divine-law ruling, the shared elements in the derivation of which the discipline of jurisprudence undertakes to determine. The divine-law ruling is the legislation emanating from God Most High to organize the life of a human being. The divine-law **articulations** in the Qur'ān and **sunna** make a ruling manifest and reveal it, but they are not the legal ruling itself.

In this light it would be a mistake to define the divine-law ruling with the formulation well-known among the early specialists in jurisprudence, since they used to define it as "divine-law articulation associated with the actions of **legal agents**." For the articulation reveals the ruling, but the ruling proper is that which the articulation signifies.

Moreover, the ruling of divine law is not always associated with the actions of legal agents but is sometimes associated with their identities [as for example being husband or wife] or with externalities pertaining to them [such as ownership], because the goal of divine-law rulings is the organization of the life of humankind. This goal, just as it is achieved by articulation associated with the actions of legal agents such as the articulation: "Pray," and "Fast," and "Don't drink wine," similarly it is achieved by an articulation associated with their identities or with other things which enter into their lives, such as rulings and articulations which organize the marital relationship and consider a woman a wife to her husband under certain specific conditions, or organize the relationship of ownership and consider a person as an owner of property under certain specific conditions. For these rulings are not associated with the actions of legal agents. Rather, the marital relationship is a divine-law ruling associated with their legal identities, and ownership is a divine-law ruling associated with wealth. The best course, therefore, is to replace the well-known early definition with what we have said here, "A divine-law ruling is legislation emanating from God in order to organize the life of a human being, whether it be connected with his/her actions or her/his identity or other things entering into his/her life."

The Division of Rulings into Injunctive and Declaratory

In the light of what has preceded we can divide rulings into two kinds.

1. One kind is the ruling in divine law associated with a person's actions and aimed directly at his/her conduct in the various aspects of his/her life as a person, as a worshipper of God, as a member of a family and as a member of society. The divine law treats and organizes all of these aspects of life, such as the prohibition of drinking wine, the mandatoriness of prayer and of material support for certain relatives, the permissible nature of bringing unused land back into use and the mandatoriness for rulers to do justice. [Such rulings are called **injunctive rulings**.]

2. The other kind is the divine-law ruling which is not aimed directly at a person in his/her actions and conduct. This includes every ruling which legislates a specific condition which has an indirect

effect on human conduct, such as the rulings which organize marital relationships. Such rulings directly legislate a specific relation between a man and a woman but affect behavior indirectly and specify, for example, that the wife after marriage is required to behave in a certain way toward her husband; such rulings are called **declaratory rulings**.

The link between injunctive and declaratory rulings is strong, since no declaratory ruling exists without an injunctive ruling alongside it. Thus the marital relationship is a declaratory divine-law ruling alongside which there exist injunctive rulings, namely the mandatoriness of expenditure by the husband on his wife and the mandatoriness of the obedience owed by the wife to her husband. Ownership is a declaratory divine-law ruling, alongside which are found injunctive rulings, such as the prohibitedness of a non-owner disposing of property without the owner's permission, and so on.

Categories of the Injunctive Ruling

The injunctive ruling, which is the ruling associated with a person's actions and aimed directly at those actions, is divided into five categories, which are as follows:

1. "The obligatory quality of an act," which is a divine-law ruling that impels one toward an act to the degree that it is compulsory, such as the mandatoriness of prayer and the mandatoriness for someone in authority to sustain the needy.

2. "The encouraged quality of an act," which is a divine-law ruling that impels one towards something to which the ruling pertains, but to a lesser degree than making it compulsory (and therefore there always exists a **dispensation** alongside it from the Lawgiver to act contrary to it). For example, the night prayer.

3. "The prohibited quality of an act," which is a divine-law ruling that restrains one from an act unconditionally, like the prohibited qualities of usury and fornication and selling weapons to the enemies of Islam.

4. "The discouraged quality of an act," which is a divine-law ruling that restrains one from an act, but not unconditionally. So that which is discouraged in the realm of restraining from action is like that which is encouraged in the realm of direction to action, just as the prohibited in the realm of restraining from action is like the obligatory in the realm of directing to action. An example of a discouraged act is failing to fulfill a promise.

5. "The permissible quality of an act," which is [a ruling in which] the Lawgiver gives latitude to the legal agent to choose the position s/he wishes. As a result, the legal agent enjoys freedom and has the right to act or not to act.

Areas of Discussion in the Discipline of Jurisprudence

DIVISION OF THE DISCUSSION ACCORDING TO TYPES

When the jurist treats a question such as the question about the saying of the **'iqāmah** prior to the liturgical prayers, and tries to derive the ruling relevant to it, s/he first asks him/herself: what is the type of divine-law ruling associated with saying the *'iqāmah*? And if s/he comes to possess a [substantiating] argument which reveals the kind of ruling defined by the law for recitation of the *'iqāmah*, it is his/her obligation to define her/his practical position and to derive the same on this basis, so that it should be a derivation resting upon this argument.

If the jurist does not come into possession of a [substantiating] argument which specifies the kind of divine-law ruling that is associated with *'iqāmah*, then the ruling defined by law will remain uncertain to the jurist. In this case the jurist will replace the first question which he proposed with a new question, as follows: What are the [general] rules that define the practical position in the face of the uncertain ruling? These rules are called procedural principles.

An example is the **priority** of **exemption**. This principle says that any instance of making something obligatory or prohibited which is not clearly based on an argument has no implication for human conduct and one is not forced to exercise **precaution** in respect to it or to feel restricted by it. The derivation of a ruling in this situation rests on a procedural principle rather than a substantiating argument. The difference between a procedural principle and a substantiating argument is that the principle does not firmly grasp ["substantiate"] the actual state of things but only defines a practical duty towards it. However, it is one method of derivation and thus we may subdivide the process of derivation into two types. The first is derivation based upon a substantiating argument, like the derivation obtained from a prooftext which indicates the divine-law ruling. The second is derivation based upon the procedural principles such as the derivation obtained from the priority of exemption.

Since the discipline of jurisprudence came into existence in order to know the commonly shared elements in the process of derivation, it supplies both types of derivation with their commonly shared elements. On this basis we subdivide jurisprudential discussions into two types. We speak in the case of the first type about the commonly shared elements in the process of legal derivation which are drawn from substantiating arguments for the ruling. In the second case we speak of the commonly shared elements in the process of legal derivation which are drawn from the procedural principles.

[PROBATIVITY OF ASSURANCE IS] THE ELEMENT COMMON TO BOTH TYPES

There is one shared element among the commonly shared elements in the procedure of derivation which enters into all processes of derivation in both its types, that based on a substantiating argument and that based on a procedural principle. This element is the probativity of **assurance**. We mean by assurance the disclosure of a certain affair to a degree which **doubt** does not degrade.

The meaning of probativity of assurance is summed up in two things:

1. One is that if the servant is involved in disobeying his/her master as a result of acting according to his/her assurance and belief, his master has no right to punish him/her, and the servant has an excuse for disobedience to the master on the basis that he acted according to his own assurance. For example, if the servant is mistakenly assured that the drink before him/her is in reality not wine and so he drinks it, relying on his assurance even though the drink is in fact wine, then the master has no right to punish him/her for drinking it as long as s/he has relied on his/her assurance. This is one of the two aspects of the probativity of knowledge, and it is called the aspect of **exculpatoriness**.

2. The other aspect is that the servant when s/he is involved in disobedience to the master as a result of his abandoning an action in spite of his/her assurance [that it must be done], then the master has the right to punish him/her and to advance his/her assurance as evidence against him. Thus, if the servant is assured that the drink before him/her is wine and then drinks it and it is in reality wine, then the master has the right to punish him/her for his/her disobedience, because the servant had knowledge of the prohibited nature of wine but drank it and so s/he will not be excused in that matter. This is the second aspect of the probativity of assurance and it is called the aspect of **inculpatoriness**.

It is self-evident that probativity of assurance in this sense which we have described is something that no process of deriving a divine-law ruling can do without, because the jurist always brings a result from the process of derivation, which is knowledge of the practical position before the divine law and the determination of that position on the basis of either a [substantiating] argument or a procedural principle. In order that this result be effective one must have prior acknowledgment of the probativity of assurance, since were assurance not evidence [for or against the actor] and were it not sound to offer it as an argument of the master against the servant and of the servant against the master, then the result which the jurist would bring forth from the process of derivation would be null. This is so because the jurist's act [of derivation] is in itself not evidence [for or against anyone]. So in any process of derivation the element of the probativity of assurance must enter in order that the process bear fruit and that the jurist bring forth a positive result. By virtue of this, the probativity of assurance has become the most general of the commonly shared jurisprudential elements and the broadest of them in scope.

The probativity of assurance is not just a commonly shared element in the processes of the derivation by the jurist of the ruling defined by the law. Rather it, in reality, is a basic condition for the study by the specialist in jurisprudence of the commonly shared elements themselves. Thus, when, for example, we study the question of the probativity of traditions or the probativity of the prima-facie sense in common usage, we make such an attempt precisely to obtain knowledge of the true situation [before the law] in that question. So if knowledge and assurance were not evidence, then what point would there be in studying the probativity of traditions or of the prima-facie sense in common usage?

For, by their discussions the jurist and the specialist in jurisprudence both seek to attain knowledge of a conclusion in legal understanding: namely, [for the jurist] "the definition of the practical position before the law;" or [for the specialist] knowledge of what is, in jurisprudential terms, "the commonly shared element." So, without prior acknowledgment of the probativity of knowledge and assurance the discussions of both become futile and useless. The probativity of assurance is firmly established by the judgment of **reason**; for reason judges that the Master, may He be praised, has the right to claim the obedience of a human in all the obligations owed to the Master and in all the injunctions and commandments and prohibitions which s/he learns about. So if a human learns of a compulsory ruling from the Master which is of "obligatory" or "prohibited" nature, then that compulsory ruling from the Master enters within the scope of the right of obedience, and it becomes the claim of the Master against the human that s/he comply with that compulsory nature of which s/he has learned. If s/he falls short in that, or has not fulfilled the claim to obedience, s/he is worthy of punishment. This is the aspect of inculpatoriness [one of the two aspects] of the probativity of assurance.

From another point of view reason also judges that a human, assured of the absence of compulsory duty, has a right to act as pleases him/herself. If the compulsory duty is established in reality, [given that the legal agent is mistakenly assured to the contrary] it is not the right of the Master to claim obedience from the human. Nor is it possible for the Master to punish him for his disobedience as long as the human is assured of the absence of the compulsory duty. In the discussion of the probativity of assurance this is the aspect of exculpatoriness.

Just as reason comprehends the probativity of assurance, so too it comprehends that its probativity cannot be divorced from assurance but is [inseparably] linked to it. It is not possible even for the Master to strip assurance of its probativity and to say that if you are assured of the absence of compulsory duty then you are not excused; or to say that if you are assured that a compulsory duty exists, you have the right to neglect it. All this is impossible according to the judgment of reason, because the aspect of exculpatoriness and the aspect of inculpatoriness cannot be separated from assurance under any condition whatsoever. Such is the meaning of the jurisprudential principle advocating the impossibility that the Lawgiver should deter one from acting according to assurance.

You might say that this jurisprudential principle means that if the servant becomes entangled in a mistaken belief and so gains assurance that the drinking of wine is lawful, then it is not the Master's right to warn her/him of the mistake. The answer is that the Master is capable of warning the servant of the mistake and of informing the servant that wine is not permitted, because that would cause the [mistaken] assurance to fall away from the mind of the servant and to restore him/her to that which is correct. The jurisprudential principle mentioned above only confirms the impossibility that the Master should deter one from acting according to assurance as long as the assurance remains firmly established [in the mind of the servant]. In the case of assurance concerning the lawfulness of drinking wine it is possible for the Master to cause the servant's assurance to cease. But it is impossible that He deter the servant from acting according to assurance and that He punish him/her on that basis as long as his/her assurance remains firmly established and his/her conviction of its lawfulness stands.

TYPE ONE: SUBSTANTIATING ARGUMENTS

An argument that the jurist relies upon in derivation of a divine-law ruling either leads to knowledge of the ruling or it does not. In the first case the argument is assured and gains its legal character and its probativity from the probativity of assurance, because the [substantiating] argument in this case leads to assurance concerning the ruling, and assurance is evidence according to the judgment of reason. Therefore it is incumbent on the jurist to construct his/her derivation of the divine-law ruling on the basis of such an argument. One example [of an assured divine-law argument] is the maxim which states: "Whenever something is mandatory that which is preliminary to it is also mandatory." So this maxim is considered to be an assured argument for the mandatoriness of ablution in its character as a **necessary preliminary** to prescribed prayer.

In the second case, the [substantiating] argument is **deficient** because it is not assured. Yet a deficient argument, if the Lawgiver rules in favor of its being evidence and orders reliance upon it in the process of derivation in spite of its deficiency, becomes as good as an assured argument and it becomes incumbent on the jurist to rely upon it. An example of a deficient argument which the Legislator has made evidence is the tradition related by a [single] reliable authority. For a tradition from a single reliable authority does not lead to knowledge [as reason would judge] because of the possibility of error or the possibility that it may be anomalous [because it disagrees with what is related by other reliable authorities]. It is a conjectural and deficient argument. The Lawgiver, however, has made it evidence and ordered that it be followed and be assented to. Thus it is raised by virtue of this [divine ruling] to the level of an assured argument.

When the Lawgiver has not ruled in favor of the probativity of a **deficient argument**, it is not evidence [at all] and reliance upon it in derivation is not permissible, because it is a deficient argument possibly subject to error. We may be in doubt and not know whether the Lawgiver has made a deficient argument evidence or not, as we do not have a [substantiating] argument which either confirms its divine-law probativity or denies it. At such a time we must have recourse to a general principle that the experts in jurisprudence have stipulated for such an occasion. This principle says: "Any deficient argument is not evidence as long as the opposite [*sc.*, the claim that this particular type of deficient argument does count as evidence] is not confirmed by a substantiating divine-law argument ." This is the meaning of what is said in the discipline of jurisprudence, "As for **conjecture**, the presumption is its non-probativity, except for that conjecture which departs [from the presumption] because of the presence of an **assured** argument." We draw the conclusion from this that a substantiating argument worthy of being relied upon in the study of the divine law is either an assured argument [in its own right] or else a deficient argument whose probativity in divine law has been established by an assured argument.

SUBDIVISIONS OF THE DISCUSSION

The substantiating argument concerning a legal question, whether it be assured or not, is divided into two divisions:

1. The first is the divine-law argument [proper]. By it we mean everything that emanates from the Lawgiver which has **signification** for the divine-law ruling and that includes the Noble Book and the sunna. The latter consists of what an infallible person said or what he did or what he tacitly consented to.

2. The second division is the rational argument, by which we mean the propositions which reason grasps and from which it is possible to derive a divine-law ruling, like the rational proposition which holds that rendering something obligatory requires the rendering of its necessary preliminary obligatory.

The first division [*i.e.*, the divine-law argument proper] is in its turn divided into two subdivisions:

1(a) The verbal divine-law argument, which is the speech of the Lawgiver whether it be found in the Book or the sunna.

1(b) The non-verbal divine-law argument such as the action of an infallible person and his/her implicit approval; that is, his/her remaining silent concerning the action of another in a way which indicates his/her acceptance.

We need to know three things concerning the first division in both of its subdivisions.

First is the [linguistic] signification of the divine-law argument and the fact that it is significant of something [intelligible] according to the prima-facie meaning in common usage.

Second is the probativity of that signification and that prima-facie meaning and the mandatoriness of reliance upon it.

Third is that [we must know that] the argument genuinely emanates from the Lawgiver.

On this basis the discussion concerning the first division is distributed into three discussions. The first discussion is concerned with the definition of signification. The second discussion is concerned with establishing the probativity of any signification and any prima-facie meaning [the verbal divine-law argument] has. The third discussion is concerned with establishing that the argument emanates from the Lawgiver.

1. THE DIVINE-LAW ARGUMENT

A. The Verbal Divine-Law Argument ("Signification")

Introduction

Since the signification of a verbal argument is associated with the general linguistic system of signification, we find it preferable to prepare for the discussion concerning the signification of verbal arguments through a summary study of the nature of **lexical** signification and the way it comes into being along with a general examination of it.

What "Designation" and "Lexical Connection" Are

There exist in every language connections between a group of utterances and a group of meanings. Each utterance is associated with a particular meaning in a way that causes us, whenever we form a mental image of the utterance, to transfer our minds immediately to a mental image of the meaning. This conjunction between **conceptualizing** the utterance and conceptualizing the meaning and transfer of the mind from the one to the other is what we name signification. So when we say, "The word 'water' signifies a particular liquid," we mean by this that the conceptualization of the word 'water' leads to the conceptualization of that particular liquid. We call the utterance "signified" and the meaning "significance." On this basis we know that the tie between the conceptualization of the utterance and the conceptualization of the meaning to a certain degree resembles the connection which we witness in our everyday life between fire and heat or between the rising of the sun and light. For just as fire leads to heat and the rising of the sun leads to light, similarly the conceptualization of the utterance leads to the conceptualization of the meaning. For this reason it is possible to maintain that the conceptualization of the utterance is a cause of the conceptualization of the meaning just as fire causes heat and sunrise causes light, except that the realm of the causal connection between the conceptualization of the utterance and the conceptualization of the meaning is the mind, whereas the realm of the tie of causation between fire and heat, or sunrise and light, is the external world.

The basic question in respect to this connection created in language between utterance and meaning is the question of the source of this connection and the manner in which it comes into being. For how is a tie of causality formed between utterance and meaning? How did conceptualization of the utterance become a cause of the conceptualization of the meaning in spite of the fact that the utterance and the meaning are two separate things that are utterly different? In answer to this fundamental question two lines of reasoning are usually mentioned in the discipline of jurisprudence, the first line being based on the connection of an utterance with its meaning growing out of the nature of the utterance itself, just as the connection of fire with heat grows from the nature of fire itself. Thus for example, the utterance "water" would be said by virtue of its nature to have a connection with the particular meaning which we understand from it. For this reason, this line of reasoning confidently asserts that the signification of a certain meaning is intrinsic and not acquired through any external cause.

This line of reasoning is incapable of fully explaining the situation, because, were the utterance's signification of the meaning and its connection with it intrinsic and not arising from any external reason, and if the utterance alone by its nature impelled the human mind to conceptualize the meaning, then why is a non-Arab incapable of making the transition to conceptualizing the meaning "water" at the time of conceptualizing the word *al-mā'*? Why is it necessary to learn the Arabic language in order for one's mind to make the transition to the meaning upon hearing the Arabic word and conceptualizing it? This is an indication that the connection that exists in our minds between the conceptualization of the utterance and the conceptualization of the meaning does not grow from the nature of the utterance, but rather from some other cause which requires that one master the language. Therefore signification is not intrinsic.

As for the other line of reasoning, it rightly denies intrinsic signification and assumes that the lexical connections between the utterance and the meaning originated in every language at the instance of some first person or first persons who invented that language and spoke in it, because they specified specific utterances for particular meanings. As a result of this specification, the utterances acquired connections with those meanings and each utterance came to signify a particular meaning.

That specification which those ancient people practiced and from which signification results is called **designation**. The practitioner of it is the "designator." The utterance is the "designated." The meaning is the "object of designation."

In truth this line of reasoning, even though it is right in denying intrinsic signification, nevertheless advances only a short step toward solving the fundamental problem, which persists even after accepting the hypothesis which the proponents of this view put forward. For if, along with them, we hypothesize that the connection of causality originated as a result of an act which the founders of language undertook when they specified each utterance for a particular meaning, then we must ask what kind of act it was which these founders undertook.

We will find that the problem does not cease to exist, because as long as there does not exist an intrinsic connection, or any prior association between utterance and meaning, how then was the founder of language able to create a tie of causality between two things between which there is no connection? Is the founder's mere specification of [a meaning for] the utterance and his assigning the utterance to the meaning sufficient to be a cause for the conceptualization of the meaning, to make it become a cause for conceptualization of the meaning in reality?

We all know that neither the founder [the coiner of an expression] nor anybody else can make out of the redness of the red ink with which he writes a cause for the heating of water, not even were he to repeat the attempt a hundred times, saying "I have singled out the redness of the ink with which I write to be a cause for the heating of water." Then how could he ever succeed in making an utterance be a cause for the conceptualization of [his] meaning [by somebody else] by merely designating it for that purpose without any prior connection between the utterance and the meaning? Thus we face the same problem we faced in the first instance. It is not sufficient for the solution of this problem to explain the connection of an utterance with its meaning on the basis of some activity undertaken by some [individual] founder of language. Rather, we must understand the content of the [whole] process in order to know how the connection of causality arose between two things which had no connection.

The proper solution of the problem is to understand that the connection of causality that exists in language between utterance and meaning is in agreement with one of the general laws of the human mind. The general law is that when the conceptualization of one of two things is accompanied numerous times in the human mind by the conceptualization of the other, even if only by coincidence, a connection arises between the two, and conceptualization of one becomes a cause for the mind's transference to the conceptualization of the other.

An example of this in our everyday lives is that we live with two friends who never part in the various situations of their life and we always find them together. After that, if we see one of the two friends alone or hear his name, our mind hastens to conceptualize the other friend, because seeing them together repeatedly has created a connection in our conceptualizing faculty. This connection makes our conceptualization of one a cause of conceptualizing the other.

It is sometimes sufficient for the thought of one of two things to be associated with the thought of the other only once for a connection to arise between the two. This happens when two concepts are associated in a striking circumstance. For example, if a person travels to a country and is stricken with a bad case of malaria then cured of it and returns home, that conjunction of malaria and his trip to that country may produce a connection between the two: whenever he conceptualizes that country, his mind moves to conceptualizing malaria.

If we study the connection of causality between utterance and meaning on this basis, the difficulty disappears, since we can explain this connection by describing it as a result of the association of the conceptualization of a meaning with the conceptualization of an utterance in a form that is repeated or in a circumstance that makes an impression, a thing which leads to the existence of a connection between the two, as occurred in the cases mentioned above.

It still remains for us to ask [exactly] how the conceptualization of an utterance became associated with a specific meaning on repeated occasions or in circumstances that make an impression, producing the existence of a lexical connection between the two.

The answer to this question is that some utterances have been spontaneously associated with specific meanings on numerous occasions and so a lexical connection has arisen between the two. The word "ah" may be of this variety, since human beings by their nature have been accustomed to uttering it from their mouths whenever they feel pain. In this way the word "ah" has become associated in their minds with the idea of pain, and whenever one hears the word "ah" one's mind moves to the idea of pain.

It is probable that before any language existed among humankind, these connections which exist between utterances of the type "ah" and their meanings had attracted human attention, as a result of the spontaneous connection between the two. In this way humankind began to create new connections between utterances and meanings. Utterances were joined with meaning by a conscious and intentional process in order that there exist a connection of causality between the two. Proper names of persons are the best example of this, for when you wish to call your son "'Alī" you join the name "'Alī" to your new son in order to create a lexical connection between them; and the name "'Alī" becomes the signifier of your son. This activity of yours is called designation. Designation is the activity by which you join an utterance with a meaning, as a result of which the mind always leaps to the meaning upon conceptualizing the utterance.

On this basis, we are able to compare designation with what you do when you ask about an eye doctor and you are told that he is Jābir; then you wish to plant his name in your memory and cause yourself to recall it whenever you wish. So you attempt to associate him with something close to your mind and, for example, you say, "Yesterday I read a book which made a great impression on me, the author of which is named Jābir; so let me always remember that the name of the eye doctor is the name of the author of that book." In this way you create a special association between the author of the book and the doctor Jābir, and thereafter you are able to recall the name of the doctor when you conceptualize that book. This method of creating an association does not differ essentially from the use of designation as a means to create a lexical connection.

On this basis we know that among the results of designation is the immediate occurrence of the meaning designated for the utterance, and its spontaneous suggestion to the mind, by merely hearing the utterance, on account of this connection which designation has established. Hence one can infer that designation is present by virtue of there being spontaneous suggestion in the mind. One can take spontaneous suggestion as a sign that the spontaneously suggested meaning is the meaning designated for the utterance, because the effect reveals the [necessary existence of the] cause. Hence, spontaneous suggestion is counted among the signs of literal meaning.

What is "Use"?

After the utterance has been designated for a meaning, the conceptualization of the utterance becomes a cause for the conceptualization of the meaning. At that moment the time of benefiting from these lexical connections which subsist between the two comes. So if you wish to convey a certain meaning to someone else and cause him/her to conceptualize it in his/her mind, then it is possible for you to speak that utterance which has become a cause for conceptualization of the meaning. When your companion hears it, his/her mind transfers to its meaning by virtue of the connection of causality between the two. Your employment of the utterance with the intention of evoking its meaning in the mind of a listener is called "**use**." For the use of an utterance for its [designated] meaning means that a person creates an utterance in order to prepare the mind of another to transfer to its meaning. The utterance is called "that which is used" and the meaning "that for which it is used." The user's intention in the evoking of meaning in the mind of the hearer by use of an utterance is called the **intention in use**.

Every use requires the conceptualization by the user of the utterance and its meaning. However the user's conceptualization of the utterance is usually instrumental, as a mirror is used in the act of seeing, while his/her conceptualization of the meaning is like an independent and direct act of seeing. Thus the utterance and the meaning are like mirror and image. Just as you look into a mirror and are unaware of it while your entire regard is for the image, similarly you look at the utterance in the same way as if it were a mirror to the meaning while remaining unaware of the utterance with your entire regard directed to the meaning.

[Just as you interpret the image of an eye seen in a mirror as an eye in reality, whereas in fact you are seeing a reflection and have therefore made two apperceptions, first that there is an image that can be interpreted as an eye and second that this image is a direct reflection of reality, in the same way you perceive a designated form of utterance and move on mentally to identify the designated meaning of the utterance with something real. Yet normally you are aware of making only one perception not two.]

If you ask, "How do I regard the utterance while remaining unaware of it? Is this not a contradiction?" They will answer you that the mirror-like act of regarding the utterance is the act of totally absorbing the utterance in the meaning. That is to say, you perceive the utterance as dissolved in the meaning and as becoming identical with the act of regarding the meaning. This kind of regard in which one thing disappears into something else is consonant with unawareness of it.

On this basis a group of scholars, such as [Khorāsānī, died 1329/1911] the late author of *Kifāyat al-'Uṣūl*, believed in the impossibility of the use of one utterance for more than one meaning. They believed this because it would require the complete absorption of the utterance in the one meaning and in the other, and the complete absorption of one thing two times on a single occasion is not rational. One might say, "I am able to unite two meanings by creating a composite containing them together and completely absorbing the utterance while regarding that composite." The answer is that this is possible, but it is the use of the utterance in a single meaning, not in two meanings.

Literal Speech and Figurative Speech

Use is divided into **literal** and **figurative**. Literal use is the use of the utterance in the meaning designated for it between which and the utterance there exists a lexical connection by reason of the act of designation. For this reason the designated meaning is given the name "the literal meaning."

Figurative use is the use of the utterance in a meaning other than that for which it was designated, but one which resembles in some respects the meaning for which the utterance was designated. An example is the use of the word "sea" referring to a learned person with abundant knowledge because he resembles the sea in abundance and amplitude. The name "figurative meaning" is applied to a meaning which resembles the meaning designated for the utterance. The connection between the utterance and the figurative meaning is a secondary connection resulting from its primary or lexical connection with the meaning designated for it, because it grows from the resemblance existing between the meaning designated and the figurative meaning.

Literal use leads directly to its goal, which is an unconditional transfer of mind on the part of the listener to conceptualization of the meaning, because the connection of causality exists in language between the utterance and the meaning for which it was designated, guaranteeing the realization of this goal.

As for figurative speech, it does not carry the mind of the listener to the meaning, since no lexical and causal connection exists between the utterance "sea" and the learned person. So in order to realize his goal in figurative use, the user needs a context which explains his intention. If s/he says, for example "a sea of learning," the word "learning" is a context for the figurative meaning. For this reason it is usually said that figurative use requires a context, unlike literal use. We distinguish the literal meaning from the figurative meaning by the immediate suggestion of the very utterance itself, because immediate suggestion in this way reveals the designation as discussed above.

The Figurative is Sometimes Turned into the Literal

Specialists in jurisprudence have correctly observed concerning figurative use that, although in the beginning it may have required a context, when such use of the utterance in the figurative meaning with a context becomes frequent and is often repeated, a new connection exists between the utterance and the figurative meaning. The utterance as a result becomes designated for that meaning and leaves the realm of the figurative for the literal. After this, no need for the context remains. This situation is called **self-specifying designation**. The procedure of designation on the part of the original designator of meaning for utterance is, in contrast, called **specifying designation**. We are able to explain this [matter] easily in light of our method of explaining the nature of designation and lexical connection, because we have come to understand that lexical connection grows from association of the utterance with a meaning that is frequently repeated or takes place in a striking circumstance. If the utterance is used in a figurative sense very frequently, the conceptualization of the utterance is repeatedly associated with the conceptualization of that figurative meaning in the mind of the listener, and this repeated association leads to the existence of a lexical connection between the two.

The Classification of Language into Substantive and Relational Meanings

As you have read in grammar, the words of language are subdivided into nouns, verbs and particles. Nouns signify meanings which we understand from those nouns regardless of whether we have heard the noun in isolation or in the setting of speech, whereas particles have no meaning unless we have heard them in the setting of speech. That which is signified by a particle is always the relationship between **substantive** [or nominal] **meanings** considering all the different aspects of their [possible] relationship. So when we say: "The fire in the hearth is burning," "in" signifies a particular relation between the two substantive concepts which are "fire" and "hearth." The following two considerations offer evidence that the significance of particles is relationship.

1. The first is that the meaning of the particle does not appear if the particle is separated from speech. That is so only because what a particle signifies is the relation between two meanings and when no other meanings are contained in that speech there is no scope for hypothesizing the relation of the two meanings.

2. The second is that there is no doubt that what is signified in speech is interrelated in its parts and there is no doubt that this interrelated thing signified includes both the relationship and the interrelated meanings. As long as no signifier for that relationship is present it is impossible to grasp such a relationship. Otherwise meanings would come to the mind while remaining scattered without any interrelation. The noun is no signifier of such relationship; otherwise we would understand its meaning only in the context of speech, because relationship is not understandable except in the framework of interrelated meanings. In this way it is specifically established that the signifier of relationship is the particle. Particles differ corresponding to the different kinds of relationship which they indicate. If every relation means a connection between two sides, then it is accurate to say that **relational meanings** are connective and correlative, whereas substantive meanings are independent meanings. Anything which indicates a connective and correlative meaning we call in jurisprudence a "particle." Anything which indicates an independent meaning we call in jurisprudence a "noun."

As for the verb, it is composed of its matter and its form. We mean by its matter the root from which the verb is derived and we mean by its form the particular mold into which that matter is poured. The matter in the verb does not differ from any noun. Thus for the word "burns" the matter is "burning." This has a substantive object of signification. Yet the verb is not [simply] equivalent to the object signified by its matter, rather it means more than that, as is evident from the impermissibility of replacing the word "burning" with the word "burns." This shows that a [finite] verb means more than what its matter [*i.e.*, its root] means. This additional meaning arises from the form.

In this way we come to understand that the form of the verb is designated to [specify] some meaning. This meaning is not an independent substantive meaning, as is evident by the fact that, were the meaning independent, it would be permissible to substitute the noun signifying that meaning and [conversely, to substitute] for the verb the noun signifying that which is signified by the matter of the verb. Whereas we observe that the verb cannot be replaced in the **sequence of speech** by bringing together two nouns. On this basis it is firmly established that what is signified by the form [of a verb] is a connective, relational meaning, and for this reason the above-mentioned substitution is impossible. This relation that the form of the verb indicates is a relation between that which is signified by the matter and that which is signified by something else in speech such as the subject [of the verb] when we say "The fire burns." For the meaningful content of the form of the verb is the relation between "burning" and "fire."

We gather from the preceding that the verb is a compound of a noun and a particle, for its matter is a noun and its form is a particle. Hence it is accurate to say that language is subdivided into two categories: nouns and particles.

The Form of the Sentence

We have come to understand that the verb has a form which indicates a relational meaning – that is, indicates a relationship – and the same is true of the sentence also. We mean by sentence two or more words between which there is interrelationship. So when we say "'Alī is the Imam," we understand from the word "'Alī" its substantive meaning, and from the word "Imam" *its* substantive meaning. In addition to that, we understand a particular relationship between these two substantive meanings. This relationship is indicated neither by the word "'Alī" alone or by the word "Imam" alone, but it is precisely the sentence with its specific form that indicates the relationship. This fact means that the form of the sentence indicates a kind of relation, which is to say, a particle-like or relational meaning.

We conclude from what has preceded that language can be classified from an analytical point of view into two classes: one of them is the class of substantive meanings, and this class includes nouns and the infinitives of verbs. The second is the class of particle-like or relational meanings, that is to say, connectors, and it includes the particles and the forms of verbs and the forms of sentences.

The Complete Sentence and the Incomplete Sentence

When we observe sentences we find that some sentences indicate a completed meaning which can be communicated by the speaker and can be **assented** to or denied by the listener. In some incomplete sentences that does not arise and it is as if they were virtually a single word. So, when you say "the learned Mufīd," we continue to expect something, just as would be the case had you said "Al-Mufīd" and fallen silent at that point. This case is in contrast with the case in which you said "Al-Mufīd [a scholar who died in 412/1021] is learned." For in that case the sentence is completed and needs no complementation.

The underlying reason for the distinction between the complete sentence and the imperfect sentence goes back to the kind of connection which the form of the sentence and the root of the relationship indicate. The form of the incomplete sentence indicates an **integrating** relationship; that is, the descriptive element is integrated with the thing described in a way such that the combination becomes a single, particular concept and a particular unit. For this reason the incomplete sentence becomes virtually an individual word. As for the complete sentence, it indicates a non-integrating relationship in which both sides remain distinct from one another. In such a case two things between which there is a tie, such as subject and predicate, are present before the mind.

Sometimes a single sentence includes both integrating and non-integrating relations, as when we say "The learned Mufīd is a teacher." For the relation between the description and the thing described, the subject, is integrating, whereas the relation between the subject and the predicate is non-integrating. The completeness of the sentence arises from the inclusion in it of this second relationship.

If we examine the incomplete sentence and particles such as "from" and "to" with care, we find that they all indicate incomplete relationships after which it is not right to fall silent. Just as it is not permissible to say "The learned teacher ..." and say no more, similarly it is not permissible to say "The journey from al-Basrah ..." and say no more. This [kind of construction] means that the relational words and the forms of incomplete sentences all indicate integrating relationships in contrast to the form of the complete sentence, for that which is signified by these complete sentences is a non-integrating relationship regardless of whether the sentence be verbal or nominal.

The Lexical Signified and the Assentable Signified

We have said previously that the signification of an utterance for a meaning consists in the conceptualization of the utterance passing to a conceptualization of the meaning. The utterance is called "signifier" and the meaning which we conceptualize on hearing the utterance is "the signified."

This signification is lexical. By this we mean that it arises from the designation of an utterance for a meaning, because designation creates the connection of causality between the conceptualization of an utterance and the conceptualization of its meaning. It is on the basis of this connection that lexical signification arises. Hence, that which is signified is the lexical meaning of the utterance.

This signification cannot be separated from the utterance whenever we may hear it and from whatever source it may come. Thus when we hear the sentence "Truth is victorious," our minds immediately transfer to the lexical matter signified, whether we have heard it from a self-aware speaker or from a sleeper in a state of unawareness or even were we to hear it as a result of the friction of two stones. So we conceptualize the meaning of the word "truth" and the meaning of the word "victorious" and conceptualize a completed relation for which the form of the sentence has been designated. This kind of signification is consequently called conceptual signification.

Yet if we compare these situations we find that when the sentence issues from a sleeping person or is produced as a result of the friction between two stones, only the lexical matter which is signified is produced, and its effect is limited to the creation [in our minds] of conceptualizations of truth and victory and of a completed relation between them. But when we hear the sentence from a self-aware speaker, the signification does not stop at the level of conceptualization but passes beyond it to the level of being assentable, since the sentence at that point reveals psychological matters internal to the speaker. Thus from the issuance of the sentence from the speaker we infer the existence of an intention in use in his/her mind; that is, s/he wishes the lexical meaning of the word "truth" and the word "victorious" and the particular form of sentence to occur to our minds and for us to conceptualize these meanings. Similarly we also know that the speaker only wants us to conceptualize these meanings, not in order that s/he create mere conceptualizations in our minds, but rather for some purpose s/he has in mind. In the preceding example, the sentence "Truth is victorious," the underlying purpose is to inform us about the established existence of the [grammatical] predicate for the subject. For the speaker wishes from us that we conceptualize the meanings of the sentence only in order that s/he inform us of their assured existence in reality. The term **intention to be serious** is applied to this fundamental purpose in the mind of the speaker. Signification of these two matters, the intention in use and the intention to be serious, is called assentable signification, because it is a signification that reveals the intention of the speaker and calls for our assent to it, not simply for our conceptualization of it and nothing more.

In this way we know that the complete sentence has, in addition to the conceptual and lexical matter signified, two matters signified which are assentable: the first is the intention in use, since we know from the way in which the sentence issued from the speaker that s/he wants us to conceptualize the meaning of the words. The second is the intention to be serious, which is the fundamental intention by reason of which the [serious and aware] speaker desires us to conceptualize these meanings [as obtaining in the real world.] Sometimes the sentence is stripped of the second kind of object of signification, namely assentable signification. This case occurs when the sentence issues from the speaker on an occasion of jest, not on an occasion of seriousness. If the speaker only intended to create conceptualizations in the mind of the hearer for the meanings of the words in his sentences, then no intention to be serious exists on this occasion but only the intention in use.

Assentable signification is not something that is lexical, that is to say, it does not express a connection arising from a [word-coining] designation between an utterance and a signified matter subject to assent. For designation creates a connection only between the conceptualization of an utterance and the conceptualization of its meaning, not between the utterance and its signified assentable matter.

Rather, it is precisely from the disposition of the speaker that assentable signification arises, for when a human is in a state of consciousness, self-awareness and seriousness and says "Truth is victorious," his/her disposition indicates that he did not speak this sentence absent-mindedly or in jest, but spoke it only with a specific, conscious intention.

In this way we come to understand that when we hear a sentence such as "Truth is victorious," we conceptualize lexical meanings for subject and predicate because of a designation which has created a connection of causality between the conceptualization of the utterance and the conceptualization of the meaning. On the other hand, it is by the speaker's disposition that we discover the conscious intention of the speaker. The former conceptualization of ours embodies conceptual signification, whereas the latter discovery of ours [about the speaker being conscious, *etc.*] embodies assentable signification. The meaning which we conceptualize is the conceptual and lexical signification of the utterance. The intention which we discover in the speaker's mind is the assentable and psychological signification of the speaker's disposition.

Thus we discover two sources of signification. The first is language with the [system of] designations which it includes; language is the source of conceptual signification. The other source of signification is the disposition of the speaker, which is the source of assentable signification, *i.e.*, what the utterance signifies psychologically and as subject to assent. An utterance reveals the intention of the speaker only when it is produced in a state of wakefulness and consciousness and seriousness. Such a disposition [of the speaker] is the source of assentable signification. Thus we find that when an utterance emanates from the speaker in a state of sleep or absent-mindedness, it has no assentable signification or psychological significance [about the speaker's intention].

Declarative and Performative Sentences

The sentence is usually classified as declarative or **performative**. In our everyday life we sense the distinction between the two. When you speak of your sale of a book yesterday and say "I sold [*biʿtu*] the book for a dinar," you see that the sentence differs fundamentally from what you would say when you wish actually to conclude a transaction with a customer and so say "I offer to sell [*biʿtu*] you the book for a dinar." Even though the sentence in both cases indicates a self-contained relationship between selling and the seller, *i.e.*, between you and the sale, our understanding of the sentence and our conceptualization of the relationship in the first case differs from our understanding and conceptualization of the relationship in the second case [in spite of the fact that the same verb *bi'tu* is used in the same tense in both sentences]. For when the speaker in the first case says "I sold the book for a dinar," s/he conceptualizes the relationship represented in the sentence as an actual reality over which s/he possesses no power except to convey information should s/he wish to mention it. But when, in the second case, s/he says "I offer to sell the book for a dinar," s/he conceptualizes the relationship, not as an actual reality which is finished and decided, but conceptualizes it in its quality as a relationship s/he hopes to realize. We conclude from this that the **declarative sentence** is designated for the complete relationship viewed as actual reality and something finished and decided. But the **performative sentence** is designated for a complete relationship viewed as a relationship the realization of which is desired.

There are some religious scholars, such as [Khorāsānī] the late author of *Kifāyat al-'Uṣūl*, who believe that the relationship which "I sold" indicates in the declarative case and the one which "I offer to sell" indicates in the performative case are the same in the two sentences, between which no difference is found at the level of the conceptual matter signified. According to them, the difference lies at the level of assentable significance. They believe so because the seller seeks by the sentence [*bi'tu*, "I offer to sell"] to bring to the fore the consideration of transferring ownership and the performance of a contract of exchange by this means, whereas from the sentence *bi'tu* ["I sold"] the non-seller seeks by the sentence to deliver an account concerning the content of the sale. So, the assentable significance differs but the conceptual significance does not.

It is obvious that if we understand this discussion rationally we see that [this view] is only at all tenable in cases in which the same utterance is used in the two sentences, one performative and the other declarative, as in *bi'tu*. It is not possible for this discussion to apply equally when either the declarative or the performative is expressly specified. The form of the **imperative**, for example, is a performative sentence not used for recounting the occurrence of an event. The imperative indicates precisely the seeking of the occurrence [of an event]. It is not possible in this case [of the imperative] to claim that conceptual significance should not act the same way here as the conceptual significance of a declarative sentence and that the difference between the two should lie only at the level of assentable significance. The argument for the impossibility of this claim is that we sense the difference between the two sentences even when stripped of assentable significance and when heard from a speaker who is unaware of what s/he is saying.

Significations Which Jurisprudence Discusses

We can divide lexical elements from a jurisprudential point of view into commonly shared elements in the procedure of derivation, and components restricted to particular cases in such a procedure. The commonly shared elements are all linguistic instruments which enter properly into any argument, whatever the kind of subject with which this argument deals may be. An example of this is the imperative form of the verb, for it is possible to use it in relation to any subject-matter.

The particular elements in the procedure of derivation are all linguistic instruments which should only enter properly into an argument that touches upon a specific subject, and has no effect in derivation for another subject. An example is the word "charity;" for it cannot be part of any argument other than an argument which includes a ruling associated with charity. There is no association between arguments which include a ruling about "prayer," for example, and the word "charity." So for this reason the word "charity" is a particular element in the process of derivation. Accordingly, in respect to language, jurisprudence studies the first category of the lexical instrumentalities that are considered commonly shared elements in the process of derivation. It investigates what is signified by the imperative form of the verb: does it indicate obligatory duty or recommended behavior? It does not investigate what is signified by the word "charity." Also among the first category of lexical instrumentalities is the [presence of a] **conditional** particle, because it is appropriate to introduce it into the derivation of rulings from any verbal argument whatever the kind of subject associated with it may be. Thus from the prooftext saying "When the sun passes the zenith, prayer becomes obligatory" we can derive the ruling that the mandatoriness of prayer is associated with decline of the sun by the argument of the [presence of the] conditional particle. From the prooftext saying "When the new moon of the month of Ramaḍān appears, the fast becomes obligatory," we can derive the ruling that the mandatoriness of the fast is associated with the event of the new moon. For this reason jurisprudence studies the conditional particle in its quality as a commonly shared element and discusses the kind of relation which it indicates and the conclusions drawn from it in the derivation of the divine-law ruling. The same is the case with the plural form defined by the definite article, because it is a lexical instrument appropriately introduced into any verbal argument, whatever kind of subject it may be associated with.

In the following we mention some examples of these commonly shared instruments which specialists in jurisprudence study.

i. The Form of the Imperative. The imperative form of the verb means commands such as "go!", "pray!", "fast!", "strive!". It is usually considered by specialists in jurisprudence as established that lexically this form indicates the mandatoriness of something. This claim causes us to wonder whether these distinguished figures mean to advocate by their statement about the imperative form indicating mandatoriness that the imperative form of the verb indicates the same thing that the word "mandatoriness" indicates? Are the imperative form and the word "mandatoriness" synonymous? How can one make this assumption, considering that we sense inwardly that the word "mandatoriness" and the imperative form are not synonymous? Otherwise it would be permissible to substitute one for the other. As long as this substitution remains unacceptable, we know that the imperative form of the verb indicates a meaning that differs from the meaning that the word "mandatoriness" indicates. Comprehending the prevailing claim among specialists in jurisprudence that the imperative form of the verb indicates mandatoriness becomes difficult at this point.

The truth is that this claim requires analysis of what is signified by the imperative form of the verb in order for us to understand in what sense it indicates mandatoriness. When we examine the imperative verb closely we find that it indicates a relationship between the meaning of the verb and its subject, viewed as a relationship the achievement of which is desired, as is the dispatching of the legal agent toward its accomplishment. Have you seen a hunter when s/he dispatches the hunting dog to his prey? That picture in which the hunter conceptualizes the dog's going to his prey when he dispatches the dog towards it is the same picture which the imperative verb indicates. For this reason it is said in the discipline of jurisprudence that the significance of the imperative form of the verb is the "dispatching relationship."

Just as the hunter when s/he dispatches the dog toward its prey is sometimes dispatching it as a result of a strong desire to obtain that prey and an urgent wish for it, and sometimes the dispatching is from a desire that is not strong and a wish that is not urgent, similarly we sometimes imagine the dispatching relationship which the form of the imperative verb indicates as resulting from a strong desire and an urgent requirement, and we sometimes imagine it as a result of a weaker desire and a wish of lesser degree. In this light we are now able to understand the meaning of that jurisprudential claim that the form of the imperative verb indicates mandatoriness, because its meaning is that this form has been designated for the dispatching relationship in its character as a result of a strong desire and an urgent requirement. For this reason the meaning of requiring and mandatoriness are included within the picture by which we conceptualize the lexical meaning of the form upon hearing it, without the imperative verb becoming a synonym for the word "mandatoriness." The meaning of the inclusion of requiring and obligation is not that the imperative cannot acceptably be used in the realm of things that are [merely] encouraged. On the contrary, this form can often be used on occasions of recommendation just as it is used on occasions of mandatoriness. Its use on occasions of mandatoriness is a literal use, because it is a use of the form in the meaning for which the form was designated. Its use on occasions of recommendation is a figurative use which the resemblance between recommendation and obligation justifies.

The argument that the form of the imperative was designated for mandatoriness in the sense we have mentioned is its spontaneous occurrence to the mind, because what comes first to mind is the common usage, as witness the fact that in common usage the giver of a command, when s/he commands a person under his/her authority with the imperative form but the latter does not do what s/he is commanded to do, offering as an excuse "I didn't know whether this is obligatory or [only] recommended," the excuse is unacceptable: s/he is blamed for his/her failure to obey. This is so only because mandatoriness comes first to mind according to common usage of the utterance and occurs to one spontaneously. Spontaneous occurrence to the mind is a sign of literal meaning.

ii. The Prohibitive Form of the Verb. The prohibitive form is something like "Do not go!" The established view among experts in jurisprudence is that the prohibitive form indicates forbiddenness.

It is necessary that we understand this claim in a way similar to our understanding of the claim that the imperative form indicates mandatoriness, with the distinction that the prohibitive is restraining and preventing, while the imperative is dispatching and seeking [an act or acts]. The prohibitive form of the imperative therefore indicates a "restraining relationship."

All of this means that when we hear the sentence "Go!," we conceptualize a relationship between going and the person addressed. We form the conception that the speaker dispatches the person addressed towards the relationship and sends him to achieve it just as a hunter dispatches his dog toward the prey. When we hear the sentence "Do not go!," we conceptualize a relation between going and the person addressed and we form the conception that the speaker is restraining the one addressed from that relationship and holding him back from it. It is just as if the hunting dog were to chase the prey and the hunter were to try to restrain the dog. It is for this reason that we have applied the term "restraining relationship." Prohibitedness enters into what is signified by the prohibitive verb form in the same way as mandatoriness enters into what is signified by the imperative. Let us return to the example of the hunter: we find that when the hunter restrains his/her dog from pursuing the prey, sometimes such restraint could be a result of a strong dislike of the dog's pursuit of the prey, and at other times a result of mild dislike. This is entirely similar to the way in which we conceptualize the restraining relationship of which we have spoken, for we sometimes conceive it to arise from a strong dislike of the thing forbidden and at other times it arises from a mild dislike.

In this light the meaning of the claim that the prohibitive form indicates prohibitedness is that the form was designated for the restraining relationship in its character as a result of strong dislike; and this is prohibitedness. So prohibitedness is included within the conception by means of which we conceive the lexical meaning of the prohibitive form upon hearing it. The argument that the prohibitive form has been designated and established for this meaning in this way is spontaneous occurrence to the mind, as has previously been mentioned concerning the imperative form. At the same time the prohibitive form may be used on occasions when discouragement is intended, and one is prohibited from the thing discouraged because of the similarity existing between discouragement and prohibition. Its use on occasions of things discouraged is a figurative use.

iii. Absolute Expression. The explanation of such expression is that when a person wishes to order his child to respect his Muslim neighbor s/he normally is not content to say to him/her "Respect your neighbor" but says "Respect your Muslim neighbor." But if s/he wants his/her child to respect his/her neighbor whatever his/her religion then s/he says "Respect your neighbor," and uses the word in an absolute sense; that is, s/he does not qualify it with a particular description. It is then understood from his/her speech that the imperative is not applied specifically to the Muslim neighbor but comprehends the non-believing neighbor as well. This comprehensiveness we understand as a result of the mention of the word "neighbor" stripped of qualification. This is called **absolute expression**, and the utterance in this case is called "absolute."

On this basis divesting the word of verbal qualification is considered a sign of the comprehensiveness of the ruling. An example of this from a divine-law prooftext are the words of God Most High, "God has made trading lawful." Here the word "trading" has occurred in speech stripped of any qualification. So this absolute expression indicates the comprehensiveness of the ruling for the permissibility of all kinds of trading.

Yet how the mention of the word in speech without qualification became a sign of comprehensiveness and what the origin of this signification is cannot be discussed in detail at this level. But we can say in brief that the prima-facie disposition of the speaker when s/he has an inner desire which impels him/her to speech is that s/he is in a position to set forth the completeness of that desire. So when s/he says "Respect your neighbor" and his desired meaning is the Muslim neighbor in particular, s/he is not content with what s/he has said but follows it normally with something which indicates the qualification of being Muslim. In any case in which s/he does not add something that indicates qualification we recognize that this qualification is not included in his/her desire since, were it included and yet s/he were silent about it, then that would contradict his prima-facie disposition, which necessarily means that he is in a position to explain the entirety of his judgment in speech. So by this inference we discover the absolute nature of the expression from silence and the absence of mention of any qualification. This is interpreted through the "context of wisdom [or rationality]."

iv. Particles of Generality. An example of a particle of generality is "every" when we say "Respect every person of moral integrity." This is so because s/he who commands, when s/he wants to indicate the comprehensiveness of his/her ruling and its generality, is sometimes satisfied with absolute expression and the mention of the word without qualification as we have previously described. In this case s/he says: "Respect [your] neighbor." But sometimes s/he wishes an increased emphasis on generality and comprehensiveness, and so employs a specific particle to signify that. Thus s/he says, in the previous example for instance, "Respect every neighbor." Then the listener understands from this a greater emphasis on generality and comprehensiveness, and for this reason the word "every" is considered one of the particles of generality because it is designated for that purpose in language. An utterance, the generality of which the particle indicates, is called "general." Such an utterance is considered as "added-to by a particle," because the particle of generality has been added to it and made it general.

We conclude from this that an indication of generality is achieved in one of two ways. The first is negative and it is absolute expression, that is, mention of the word without restriction. The second is positive and it is the use of a particle of generality such as "every" and "all" and "the entirety" and similar expressions.

Specialists in jurisprudence have disagreed concerning the form of the plural preceded by the definite article, such as "the jurists" or "the contracts." Some say that this form itself is also one of the particles of generality just like the word "every." So when the speaker wishes to establish a ruling for all individuals and to indicate in a positive way generality for any [unmistakable] plural like "jurists" s/he adds the definite article and says, "Respect the jurists" or "Fulfill the contracts."

Other specialists believe that the plural with the definite article is not one of the particles of generality, and that we only understand the comprehensiveness in the ruling when we hear the speaker say, for example, "Respect the jurists," because of the absolute expression and the divestment of the word of qualifications, not because of the addition of the definite article to the plural – that is, by a negative, not a positive, method of arriving at the conclusion. So there is no difference between saying "Respect the jurists" and "Respect the jurist." Just as our understanding relies in the second sentence on absolute expression for its comprehensive meaning, the same is the case in the first sentence. So [both] the singular and the plural with the definite article only indicate comprehensive meanings in a negative way [*i.e.*, by the absence of qualifications].

v. The Particle of the Conditional. The particle of the conditional is a word such as "when" in our saying "When the sun passes the zenith, pray" and "When you enter a state of ritual consecration for the pilgrimage, do not use scent!" The sentence to which the particle of the conditional is added is a conditional sentence. It differs in its linguistic task from other sentences in which a conditional particle is not found. Other sentences establish a relationship between one word and another, like the relationship of the predicate to the subject in a categorical proposition [*i.e.*, a statement about the members of two classes and their relation to one another]. A conditional sentence, however, ties together two sentences, the clause of the condition, or protasis, and the clause of consequence, or apodosis. Because of this tie of conditionality both sentences are transformed from a complete sentence to an incomplete sentence, and the complete sentence is the combination of the conditional sentence and its complement.

If we observe the two preceding examples of the conditional sentence we find that the condition in the first example is the declining of the sun from the zenith, and in the second example it is the entering a state of ritual consecration for the pilgrimage. As for what is made conditional, it is the significance of the sentence "Pray!" or "Do not use scent!" If the significance of "Pray!" in its quality as an imperative form is mandatoriness and the significance of "Do not use scent!" in its quality as a prohibitive form is forbiddenness, as has been discussed previously, then we know that that which has been made conditional is mandatoriness or prohibitedness respectively, that is to say, the divine-law ruling [as to the nature of the situation]. The meaning of saying that the divine-law ruling is conditional on the declining of the sun or on entering a state of ritual consecration for the pilgrimage [in which the use of perfume is forbidden] is that the ruling depends on the declining of the sun or entering into a state of ritual consecration and [the divine-law ruling] is restricted by that [condition]. That which is restricted ceases to have force when the restriction ceases.

From this it follows that the conditional particle indicates the disappearance of a legal ruling in case of the disappearance of a condition, because such disappearance is a result of the sentence's signifying the restriction of the divine-law ruling and its making the ruling conditional. Our saying "When the sun passes the zenith, pray!" indicates the non-mandatoriness of prayer before noon. Our saying "When you enter the state of ritual consecration for the pilgrimage, do not use scent!" indicates the non-prohibited nature of scent in the situation of not entering a state of ritual consecration for the pilgrimage. In this way the conditional sentence possesses two significances, one positive and one negative.

The positive significance is the establishment of the consequence at the same time as the establishment of the condition. The negative significance is that the consequence ceases when the condition ceases.

The positive significance is called the **explicit** significance of the sentence; and the negative, the **implicit**. Of every sentence which has this sort of negative significance it is said, according to common jurisprudential usage, that the sentence or proposition contains an implicit significance.

A certain specialist in jurisprudence has laid down a general rule about this negative significance in language, and has said, "Every lexical particle which indicates the restricted nature of a ruling and its delimitation must have a negative significance, since the particle indicates the disappearance of the ruling outside the scope of the bounds designated for the ruling." The conditional particle is considered one of the corroborating instances of this general rule because it indicates the delimitation of the ruling by a condition.

Also among the corroborating instances of this general rule is the particle of **limit** when, for example, you say: "Fast until the sun sets." For "fast" here is an imperative verb indicating mandatoriness and "until," in its quality as a particle of **limit**, has indicated the fixing of a boundary and a limit for this mandatoriness which the imperative form indicates. The meaning of [sunset] being a limit to [the obligation to fast] is that it restricts [the ruling], which indicates the cessation of the obligation of fasting after sunset. This is the negative significance to which the term implicit has been applied. The negative significance of the conditional sentence is called the "implicit meaning of the condition" just as the negative significance of the particle of limit, such as "until" in the preceding example, is called "the implicit meaning of the limit."

But when somebody says "Respect the righteous poor person," that does not signify a restriction to the effect that an unrighteous person should not be respected, because this restriction is not a restriction of the ruling [as a whole] but rather an epithet and a restriction applying [only] to the poor person. The poor person is the subject of the ruling, not the ruling itself. As long as a restriction does not refer directly to the ruling, it has no signification for the implicit meaning. Hence it is said that there is no implicit meaning for the epithet, by which is meant words like the word "righteous" in this example.

The Probativity of the Prima-Facie Meaning

When we confront a divine-law argument it is important that we do not explain it merely in relation to its lexical and conceptual significance. Rather, it is important to explain it in relation to its assentable significance in order that we know what the Lawgiver intends by it. Frequently we observe that an utterance is correct in several lexical and commonly understood significations. How are we able to decide what the speaker intended on the basis of what he said?

At this point we can make use of two aspects of "prima-facie" meaning. The first is the prima-facie meaning of the utterance at the stage of conceptual signification for a specific meaning. The meaning of "prima-facie" at this stage is that this prima facie meaning rather than other meanings is the first to be conceptualized by a person on hearing the utterance. This meaning is the closest to the utterance from the point of view of language. The second is the prima-facie disposition of the speaker, in that what s/he means is in accordance with the prima-facie sense of the utterance at the stage of conceptual signification. That is to say that s/he intends the meaning closest to the utterance lexically considered [*i.e.*, closest to the originally designated and literal sense]. This is what is called "prima-facie accordance between the 'category of assertion' and the 'category of reality.'" It is a matter agreed upon in jurisprudence that the prima-facie disposition of the speaker in intending the meaning nearest to the utterance constitutes evidence.

The meaning of the "probativity of the prima-facie sense" is that the jurist is to adopt that sense as a basis for the explanation of a verbal argument in that light. So we should always assume that the speaker intended the meaning closest to the utterance* in the general lexical system, accepting his prima-facie disposition.

Therefore the probativity of the prima-facie sense is called "the priority of the prima-facie sense" because it makes the prima-facie sense a root principle for explanation of a verbal argument.

In the light of this conclusion we are able to recognize why we have concerned ourselves in the preceding discussion with determining the

* [Footnote in original] We do not here mean by language and the general lexical system an understanding of language in contrast to common usage. Rather we mean the system in fact existing for the signification [of meaning] for utterances, whether it be on the primary [lexical] level or the secondary level [of common usage].

lexical significance closest to the word and determining the prima-facie meaning of the word according to the general lexical system. Nevertheless, the important matter at the moment of interpretation of the verbal argument is the discovery of what the speaker intended in terms of meaning by his/her utterance, not what is the meaning nearest to the utterance in language. For, in light of the priority of the prima-facie sense, we understand that the tie between discovery of the meaning intended by the speaker and determination of the lexical significance closest to the word is extremely tight, because the priority of the prima-facie sense judges that the meaning that the speaker intends by the utterance is the same as the closest lexical significance, that is to say, the prima-facie meaning of an utterance lexically considered. So, in order to know the meaning intended by the speaker it is necessary that we know the meaning closest to the utterance lexically in order that we judge it to be the meaning intended by the speaker.

The argument for the probativity of the prima-facie sense consists of two prior premises. The first is that the behavior of the companions of the Prophet and of the Imams was based on acting both according to the prima-facie meanings of the Qur'ān and sunna, and according to their taking these things prima facie as a basis for understanding them, as is plainly evident historically from the way they acted and believed.

The second is that infallible persons saw and heard others acting in this way and did not object to it at all. This fact indicates the soundness of this approach according to the divine law; otherwise they would have deterred people from it. By this means it has been established that the Lawgiver has endorsed behavior based on acting according to the prima-facie sense. Such is the meaning of the probativity of the prima facie in divine law.

Applications of the Principle of the Probativity of the Prima-facie Sense to Verbal Arguments

In what follows we examine three situations for the application of the principle of the probativity of the prima facie.

1. The first is that in which the utterance in the argument has a single, unique meaning in language and it is not appropriate to use [that utterance] to signify any other meaning in the common-usage lexical system. The general principle that is prescribed [*i.e.*, the probativity of the prima facie] in this situation is that the utterance refers to its unique meaning; it is said that the speaker intended that meaning because the speaker always intends by the utterance the meaning defined for it in the common-usage lexical system. In a situation like this the argument is considered clear in its meaning and explicit in its specification

2. The second [situation] is that in which the utterance has more than one meaning, equally connected with the utterance according to the common-usage lexical system, as in the case of a homonym. In this situation it is not possible to specify the intended meaning of the utterance on the basis of that rule, since no one meaning is closest to the utterance lexically so that the rule should be applied. The argument in this case is indeterminate.

3. The third [situation] is the case in which an utterance has more than one meaning in language, but one meaning is lexically nearer to the utterance than the others. An example is the word "sea", which has as its literal meaning that which is near to hand, as in "sea of water", and as its figurative meaning that which is remote, as in "sea of knowledge." So if the giver of a command says "Go to the sea every day" and we want to know which of the two meanings the speaker intended by the word "sea," we must study the **passage** in which the word "sea" occurs. We mean by "passage" all other indications that shed light on the utterance which we wish to understand, regardless of whether they be verbal, such as the words which form a single connected aggregate of speech with the utterance we want to under-

stand, or circumstantial, such as the circumstances and concomitants which surround the speech and possess signification for the designated [utterance, as for instance "the sea"].

If we do not find in the other words which occur in the context anything that contradicts the prima-facie meaning of the word "sea" it is compulsory for us to explain the word "sea" on the basis of the lexical meaning closest to it in accordance with the principle which asserts the probativity of the prima-facie sense. But we sometimes find in other parts of the passage things that do not agree with the prima-facie sense of the word "sea." An example is when the giver of a command says "Go to the sea every day and listen to its conversation with care." For listening to the speech of the sea does not agree with the lexical meaning closest to the word "sea." But, for the learned person who resembles the sea because of the abundance of his/her knowledge, it is appropriate. In this circumstance we find ourselves wondering what the speaker means by the word "sea." Does s/he intend by it "the sea of knowledge," using the argument that s/he has ordered us to listen to his/her conversation, or did s/he intend by it "a sea of water" and did not mean here by "conversation" the literal meaning of the word, but rather paying heed to the sound of the waves of the sea? In this way we hesitate between the word "sea" and its prima-facie lexical sense on the one hand, and the word "conversation" and its prima-facie lexical sense on the other. The meaning of this is that we hesitate between two images. One of them is the image of going to a surging sea and listening to the sound of its waves, which is the image which the word "sea" inspires. The other is the image of going to a learned person of abundant knowledge and listening to his/her speech, which is the image inspired by the word "conversation."

In this case we must consider the passage as a whole and in its entirety, and see which of these two images is closer to the passage according to the general lexical system. In other words, this passage, when it is presented to the mind of a person who accurately experiences language and its system, will the first or second image rush to his/her mind? For if we know that one of the images is closer to the passage in accordance with the general lexical system – let us assume it is the second – then in the case of this second image, a prima-facie understanding is created for the passage as a whole. It is our duty to explain the passage on the basis of that prima-facie image.

The word "conversation" in this example is called the **context** because it is what signifies a perfect image for the passage, and invalidates the literal sense of the word "sea" and its prima-facie sense. If the two images were equally connected with the passage, this would mean that the speech had become **indeterminate**, without any prima-facie sense. This situation would mean that no scope remains for the application of the general principle [of the probativity of the prima facie].

The Connected and Independent Context

We have come to understand that the word "conversation" in the preceding example might be the context for that sequence of words as a whole. It is called a **conjunctive context** because it is conjoined with the word "sea," which invalidates the literal meaning when [found] accompanying [the conjunctive context] in a single passage. The word which loses its literal meaning because of the context is called "contextualized."

An example of a connected context is an exception from the general, as when the giver of a command says, "Respect every poor person except sinners." The word "every" lexically has the prima-facie sense of generalization, but the word "sinners" is incompatible with this generalization. When we study the sequence of words as a whole we see that the image which this word "sinners" entails is closer to [the sense of] the passage than the image of generalization which the word "every" entails. In fact, there is no room for comparison between the two. For this reason the particle of exception [*sc.*, the word "except"] is considered to be the context for the general meaning of the passage. So the conjunctive context is everything that is conjoined with another word and that invalidates the prima-facie sense [of that word] and directs the general meaning of the passage in a direction which is in harmony with itself.

Sometimes it happens that the context with this meaning does not appear connected to the speech in question, but disjunct from it. It is called a **disjunctive context**. An example is when the giver of a command says "Respect every poor person." Then s/he says in another conversation a while later, "Do not respect the sinners among the poor." This prohibitive [verb form], had it been conjoined with the first speech, would be considered a conjunct context; yet it was disjoined from it in this example. In this light we understand the meaning of the jurisprudential rule that says "The prima-facie sense of the context takes precedence over the prima-facie sense of what is contextualized by it, regardless of whether the context be conjunctive or disjunctive."

Establishing the Source

In order that we act according to a certain speech in its quality as a divine-law argument one undoubtedly must establish that it emanates from an infallible person. There are several methods of doing so:

1. The first is from **wide-scale transmission**, which means that a large number of transmitters convey an account [about an infallible person] and each narrative from that large number constitutes [an element of weight] for the probability of the proposition, and a context for its establishment. By virtue of the accumulation of probabilities and contexts, certainty as to the emanation of the speech [from an infallible source] is achieved. The probativity of wide-scale transmission rests on the basis of its usefulness for [establishing legal] knowledge. Its probativity has no need for a divine-law promulgation or for it to be an act of human obedience [to God, seeking nearness to God].

2. Second is **consensus** and **prevalence**. The explanation of this is that when, for example, we observe the **response** of a single jurist on the mandatoriness of the application of the one-fifth tax on mines, we

find that it constitutes a context insufficient to establish the existence of a prior verbal argument [derived from a prooftext] indicating the mandatoriness [of the mine tax], because we can conceive two possible explanations of the jurist's response. The jurist in his response may have relied on, say, a verbal argument in a sound manner, but on the other hand, he may have been simply mistaken in the response. As long as we conceive both these explanations as equally likely, this response is a context which establishes [an argument] only insufficiently. When we add to it the response of another jurist on the mandatoriness of the twenty percent mine tax, the probability of the existence of a verbal argument for the ruling becomes greater as a result of the conjunction of two insufficient contexts. When we add to the two jurists a third we become even more willing to believe in the existence of this verbal argument, and so on as the number of jurists in favor of the mandatoriness of the one-fifth tax on mines increases. When the jurists have agreed universally on this response, it is called consensus, but if they only constitute a majority, it is called prevalence. So, consensus and prevalence are two methods for the discovery of the existence of a verbal argument in a number of circumstances.

The ruling of consensus and prevalence from a jurisprudential point of view means that when knowledge of a divine-law argument has been achieved by means of consensus or prevalence, adoption of this knowledge is mandatory in the process of derivation. Consensus and prevalence in this way become evidence. When consensus and prevalence [have been invoked but] do not lead to knowledge, then no consideration should be paid to either, since at that point all they would lead to is supposition. From the standpoint of divine law there is no argument for the probativity of supposition. For the basic principle is that such supposition is not probative, because that is the basic principle concerning [all] supposition, as was discussed above.

3. The third is the common practice of the religiously observant. This is the general behavior of the religious in the age of the infallible persons, such as their agreement to perform midday prayer on Friday

instead of the **Friday prayer**, or their agreement on the non-payment of the one-fifth canonical tax on an inheritance. If we divide this general behavior analytically into its separate instances, and consider each individual's behavior in isolation, we find that the behavior of any single religious individual in the age of legislation is considered a context insufficient to establish that a clear divine-law statement confirming that behavior was ever issued. At the same time we see that the behavior of that single individual may have resulted from error or negligence or even mere laxity.

If we know, for example, that two individuals in the age of legislation used to behave the same way and both prayed the midday prayer on Friday, the case for this behavior being correct is reinforced. The case continues to grow stronger as the number of examples increases until it reaches a high degree [of probability], at which point we know that that was general behavior which the great mass of pious people followed in the age of legislation, since it appears certain at this point that the behavior of all these individuals cannot have originated through error, negligence or laxity. For one or another person might fall into error, negligence or laxity, but it is not likely that this should happen to the great mass of the pious in the age of legislation.

In this way we know that the general behavior is based on a clear divine-law elucidation which indicates the possibility of performing the midday prayer on Friday, and that there is no obligation to pay the one-fifth canonical tax on an inheritance. [The principle of pious practice] leads in the great majority of cases to certainty about a divine-law elucidation when applied under certain conditions which there is no room to examine here in detail. When [pious practice] thus leads to certainty, it is evidence. When it does not yield certainty, then it is not worthy of any consideration, because there is no argument for its probativity under those circumstances.

These three methods are all based on the accumulation of probabilities and combination of contexts.

4. The fourth [method of authentication of traditions] is the **single-source account** reported by a single authority who is reliable.

We use the term single-source account for any account that does not provide us with usable knowledge. The way to judge such a report is that if the informant is reliable it is adopted and it is evidence, otherwise not. Such probativity is established on the basis of the divine law and not on the basis of reason, because it does not rest on the basis of reaching assurance but on the basis of the command of the Lawgiver to follow the account of a reliable person. Numerous divine-law arguments point to this principle, and – God willing – an exposition of them will come in the next volume. Among these arguments is the verse in the Qur'ān entitled "The Report" – "O you who believe, if a sinner come to you with a report, look into it carefully …" (*Al-Ḥujurāt* 49: 6). This verse contains a conditional sentence which expressly indicates that the obligation to inquire closely is contingent upon the coming of a sinner with a report, but it also indicates implicitly that there would be no obligation to inquire closely in the case of the arrival of a report from a non-sinner. That [contingent non-inquiry], however, is only so because of the probativity [of the report of a non-sinner]. Thus one learns from this noble verse that the report of a [single] reliable and upright person is probative.

Another argument for the probativity of the report of such a person is that the practice of the religiously observant and of reasonable people generally is based on confidence in such a report. We discover from the uniformity of pious practice on this point and the firm reliance on it of the practice of the Imams' companions and the practice of the transmitters of traditions that the probativity [of the single-person account] has been transmitted to them from the Lawgiver. All this is in agreement with what has been previously said about pious practice and about how to draw inferences using it.

B. The Non-Verbal Divine-Law Argument

The non-verbal divine-law argument is everything that emanates from an infallible person which has significance for a divine-law ruling but is not of the category of speech. Included in this is the act of an infallible person, for if the infallible person performs an act it indicates his/her permission for such an act; but if s/he abstains from an act, it indicates that it is non-mandatory. If the infallible source performs an act as a sign of his/her being obedient to God Most High, that indicates the desirable character of the act. The emanation of these kinds of behavior from an infallible person is established by the same methods as previously discussed, by which the emanation of verbal divine-law arguments is established.

Also included in the non-verbal argument is the **tacit consent** of the infallible person. It consists of his/her silence concerning behavior in his/her presence, signifying endorsement. Otherwise it would have been incumbent on the infallible person to deter the actor from his action. Thus, non-deterrence reveals endorsement and consent.

The behavior is sometimes a personal behavior in a specific circumstance, as when a person performs ablution before the Imam and wipes him/herself in the reverse direction and the Imam remains silent about his/her action. Other times it is a generic human behavior such as the **conduct of reasonable people**. Such conduct consists of the general inclination among reasonable people toward a specific course of behavior without there being any positive role on the part of the Lawgiver in creating this inclination. Examples of this include the general inclination among reasonable people to adopt the prima-facie sense of the speaker or the single-person account or to consider possession as a cause for ascribing ownership of objects that belong to no one. The conduct of reasonable people in this sense differs from the conduct of those religiously observant people of which it has been previously said that it is one of the means to disclose the emanation of a divine-law argument. For the conduct of the pious in their quality as such will usually be the product of a statement of divine law. For this reason their conduct is held to reveal such statements of divine law the way an effect reveals its cause.

As for the conduct of reasonable people, it is attributable, as we have come to understand, to a general inclination which is found among the reasonable toward a specific form of behavior, and is not the result of divine-law statement but the result of other factors and influences which condition it accordingly, including the inclinations and modes of behavior of reasonable people. On this account the general inclination which is considered to be the conduct of reasonable people is not restricted to the sphere of the pious in particular, because religiosity has not been one of the factors that creates this inclination.

In this way it becomes clear that the conduct of reasonable people does not disclose a divine-law statement in the way that the effect reveals the cause, but discloses the divine-law ruling only by means of signification by tacit consent [of the infallible person], according to the following analysis: the inclination among the reasonable toward a specific course of behavior is considered to be a mental faculty impelling them toward practicing that behavior. If the divine law is silent concerning that inclination and an infallible person has not restrained [somebody from] such behavior, even though this infallible person lived at the time of that behavior, it becomes clear that that person was pleased with and endorsed that behavior in terms of the divine law. An example of that is the silence of the divine law concerning the general inclination among intelligent people toward adopting the prima-facie sense of the speech of a speaker, and non-deterrence by infallible persons from acting accordingly. For their non-deterrence indicates that the divine law confirms this way of understanding speech, and implies that the prima-facie meaning is to be considered evidence. Otherwise, the divine law would have forbidden our acquiescing in that general inclination, and would have deterred us from [taking the prima-facie sense] within the scope of the divine law. In this way we are able to infer the probativity of the prima-facie sense from the conduct of reasonable people, in addition to our inferring it previously on the basis of the behavior of the religiously observant contemporaries of the Prophet and the Imams.

Rational Arguments: the Study of Rational Connections

When reason studies the relations between things it arrives at a recognition of numerous types of such relations. For example, it comprehends the relation of (1) contrariety, or opposition between contraries, which exists, *e.g.*, between blackness and whiteness. This relation means the impossibility of [both qualities] existing simultaneously in one body. [Reason] also comprehends the relation of (2) necessary consequence between that which causes and that which is caused. In the view of reason everything caused is necessarily subsequent to its cause and it is impossible to separate the caused from the cause; such is the case with heat in respect to fire. Reason further comprehends the relation of (3) antecedence and subsequence [or **succession in existence**], as for example, when you hold a key in your hand and you move your hand and subsequently the key moves because of that. In spite of the fact that the key in this example moves at the same instant in which your hand moves, reason comprehends the motion of the hand as being antecedent and the motion of the key as being subsequent, not from a temporal point of view but from the point of view of succession in existence. For this reason we say when we want to speak of this matter, "My hand moved then the key moved." "Then" in this instance indicates that the motion of the key is subsequent to the motion of the hand in spite of the fact that the two occur at the same time. Thus in this case the subsequence does not have anything to do with time, but arises only from succession in existence [of things] from the point of view of reason. The meaning of this is that when reason notices the motion of the hand and the motion of the key, and comprehends that the latter springs from the former, it considers the motion of the key as subsequent to the motion of the hand in its character as arising from it, and represents this subsequence by the word "then." Thus one says: "I moved my hand, and then the key moved." The term applied to this subsequence is "subsequence in logical order."

After reason has grasped such connections as these, it can use them to discover the presence or absence of something. Reason, by using the relation of contrariety between black and white, is able to establish the absence of black in a body when it knows that it is white, in view of the impossibility of blackness and whiteness coexisting in a single body. Similarly, by using the relation of necessary consequence between the caused and its cause, reason is able to establish the existence of the caused when it knows the existence of the cause, given the impossibility of separating the two. Likewise, by using the relation of antecedence and subsequence [succession in existence], reason can discover that the subsequent did not exist before the antecedent, because that would contradict its being subsequent. So if the motion of the key is subsequent to the motion of the hand in the sequence of existence, it would be impossible that the motion of the key, when the situation is thus, should exist in any form antecedent to the motion of the hand in the succession of existence.

Just as reason comprehends such relations as these between things and makes use of them to discover the presence or absence of something, similarly it comprehends the connections existing between [divine-law] rulings, and [reason] benefits from these connections in order to discover the existence or nonexistence of a ruling. For example, reason understands the contrariety between being mandatory and being prohibited the same way it understood the contrariety between black and white [in the former example]. Just as [reason] used the latter connection to reject blackness when the existence of whiteness was known, so it uses the connection of contrariety between mandatory and prohibited to reject the mandatoriness of an act known to be prohibited.

Thus we find things between which connections exist from the perspective of reason and we also find rulings between which connections exist from the perspective of reason. To the things we apply the name "the creational world." To the rulings we apply the name "the legislative world."

Just as reason can detect the existence or nonexistence of something in the creational world by means of these connections, so reason can detect the existence or nonexistence of a ruling in the legislative world by means of these connections. Accordingly, it is one of the duties of the discipline of jurisprudence to study such connections in the world of rulings in their quality as rational judgments qualified to be common elements in the process of derivation. In what follows, examples of such connections will be presented.

Subdivision of the Discussion

In the legislative world several categories of rational connections are found, namely those between:

1. one divine-law ruling and another;
2. a ruling and its **subject**;
3. a ruling and its **dependent object**;
4. a ruling and its **necessary preliminaries**;
5. different elements within a single ruling; and
6. a ruling and other external things in the purview of the creational world.

We will discuss examples of most* of these categories in what follows.

Connections Arising Between One Ruling and Another

i. The Connection between Mandatory and Prohibited. In the discipline of jurisprudence it is recognized that it is quite possible for a legal agent to perform two acts at the same time, one mandatory and the other prohibited, and so be considered obedient to God and worthy of reward in performing the mandatory act, yet disobedient to God and worthy of punishment in performing the prohibited act. An example

* [Footnote in original] That is to say, we will give examples of all but the sixth category. By this sixth category we refer to things such as necessary connections arising between rational judgments and divine-law rulings established by the axiom "Every thing that reason rules, divine law rules." Such connections arise between a divine-law ruling and something outside the purview of the legislative world, *i.e.*, a ruling of the intellect [or reason]. We have scheduled the treatment of that category for future courses.

would be to drink impure water and pay the canonical alms to the poor at the same time.

One cannot possibly describe any single act as mandatory and prohibited at the same time, because the connection between mandatory and prohibited is a connection of contrariety. One can no more combine the mandatory and the permitted in a single act than combine black and white in a single object. Payment of the canonical alms to the poor, being mandatory, cannot be prohibited at the same time. The drinking of **impure** water, being prohibited, cannot be mandatory at the same time.

So clearly (1) two distinct acts, such as paying canonical alms and drinking impure water, can be described the one as mandatory, and the other as forbidden, even when the legal agent performs them both at the same moment, whereas (2) a single act cannot be described as both mandatory and prohibited. The crucial point in this discussion for the specialists in jurisprudence is that an act may be single in its essence and existence, and yet multiple in its description and legal categorization. In such a case, is it to be counted as one act due to its being single in essence and existence, or is it to be counted as two acts due to its description and legal categorization?

For example, a legal agent might perform ablution with water that has been misappropriated from its rightful owner. The action which the legal agent thus performs, if it were viewed from the point of view of the existence of the action, would be a single thing, but if viewed from the point of view of its attributes, it would be described by two different attributes. Therefore one may say of the action "It is ablution" and at the same time say "It is misappropriation, disposing of somebody else's property without permission," and each of these descriptions is a [suitable] legal categorization. Therefore the action in question is to be accounted single in its essence and existence, but multiple when it comes to describing it and assigning it to a legal category.

On this point there are two opinions advocated by specialists in jurisprudence:

1. As long as an action remains multiple as regards description and legal categorization, it counts as two distinct acts. Just as one can describe the payment of the canonical alms to the poor as mandatory and the drinking of impure water as prohibited, so it is possible for one of the two descriptions/characterizations of the act to be "mandatory" (the legal category for ablution), while its other description is "prohibited" (the legal category for misappropriation). Those who take this view are said to advocate "the permissible conjunction of command and prohibition."
2. The other opinion insists that the action be counted as a single act on the basis of its essential unity: mere differentiation of description and legal categorization according to this view does not warrant tying the mandatory and the prohibited together in one and the same action. This view is called "the impossibility of conjoining command and prohibition."

In this way jurisprudential inquiry has been directed to the study of the plurality of description and categorization [of a single act]. Is the conjunction of mandatory and prohibited in the action of ablution with misappropriated water warranted? Or [are we to hold] that as long as an action remains single existentially and essentially, it cannot be described as being at once mandatory and prohibited?

It might be said that rulings, considered as things that arise in the inner mind of the Lawgiver, are connected with mental categories and images only, not with external reality directly. The plurality of categories and forms is sufficient to remove any difficulty, and the meaning of it is that the conjunction of command and prohibition is permissible.

It may [on the other hand] be said that rulings, although they are connected with mental categories and images, are nevertheless not connected with them by virtue of the rulings being mental images themselves, since it is clear that the Master does not will the image. Rulings are only connected with images insofar as images are expressive of external reality and mirror it. Since external reality is a unity, it is impossible that the mandatory and the prohibited be conjoined in it even through the mediation of two categories or two images.

On this basis it is said that if the multiplicity of categories is a result of the multiplicity in the external world and discloses the multiplicity of existence, then it is acceptable that command should be connected with one of two things and prohibition with the other thing; whereas, if there exists nothing but a multiplicity in the world of categories and images – which [world] is the mind – then that [conjunction of command and prohibition] is not acceptable.

ii. Does Prohibitedness Require Invalidation? The meaning of validity of contract is that the effect upon which the two contractors agreed results from it. So in a contract of sale, the sale is considered valid and effective when the transfer of ownership of the goods from the seller to the buyer, and the transfer of possession of the purchase price from the buyer to the seller, result from the contract. The sale is considered void and invalid if those exchanges do not result from it.

It is self-evident that a contract cannot be valid and invalid at the same time, because validity and invalidity are two mutually exclusive contraries like the contrariety between mandatory and forbidden.

The question is whether it is possible that a contract be both valid and prohibited. We respond in the affirmative, since there is no contrariety between validity and being prohibited, and also no necessary connection between being prohibited and being invalid, because the meaning of declaring a [type of] contract prohibited is to restrain a legal agent from effecting such a sale, whereas the meaning of the contract being valid is that if a legal agent resists such restraint and prohibition and makes a sale, legal consequences result from his selling – the property passes from seller to buyer. There is no incompatibility between a legal agent's effecting a sale that is repugnant to the Lawgiver and prohibited to [the legal agent] and the fact that legal consequences ensue when it is initiated by the legal agent. Such a case is exactly like the case with the **ẓihār** form of divorce, which is forbidden according to the divine law, but were a *ẓihār* divorce to occur, the legal consequences would nevertheless proceed from it.

An example in everyday life is that you do not want so-and-so to visit you and dislike his doing so in the highest degree. But when the thing actually happens and the visit is made, you regard it a duty on your side that the [conventional] consequences follow from his visit – you undertake to be hospitable to the visitor.

So we recognize that the fact of a transaction, that is to say, a contract of sale or the like, being prohibited does not necessarily make it invalid but is compatible with a simultaneous ruling about the validity of the contract. We differ from a number of experts in jurisprudence who hold that the prohibitedness of a transaction demands its invalidation.

As prohibition is [rationally] connected with [the validity of] a contract or transaction, similarly it may be connected with acts of devotion like the prohibition of fasting on a feast day or the prohibition of prayer for menstruating women. This kind of prohibition, however, requires that the act of devotion be null and void, unlike prohibition in the case of a transaction. That is because an act of devotion does not come to pass validly except when a legal agent performs it seeking closeness to God. After its prohibitedness becomes apparent, one cannot seek closeness to God by means of it, because closeness to God by means of something repugnant and disobedient to Him is impossible. Thus [a prohibited act of devotion] is performed in vain.

Connections Arising Between a Ruling and Its Subject

Promulgation and Actuality. When the divine law ruled that the pilgrimage is mandatory for the capable and there came the saying of God Most High, "By God, pilgrimage to the House is [incumbent] upon mankind, anyone who can [manage] a way to it" [*'Āl 'Imrān* III: 97], pilgrimage became one of the obligatory duties in Islam and its mandatoriness became a ruling established in the divine law. But if we suppose that at that time there was not a single capable person among the Muslims in whom the characteristics of "capability" were fulfilled according to the divine law, then the mandatoriness of the pilgrimage would not have applied to any individual among the Muslims because they were all not capable. The pilgrimage is an obligation only for the capable, which means that the mandatoriness of the pilgrimage is not established in this situation for any particular individual, in spite of its being a ruling established in the divine law. When one of the individuals becomes capable, the obligation is directed to him or her, and becomes established in respect to him/her.

In this light we observe that a ruling has two sorts of "being established" – one is the ruling being established in the divine law, and the other is it being established in respect to this or that individual. When, in the above cited noble verse, Islam ruled that pilgrimage is mandatory for the capable person, this ruling was established in the divine law even if no capable person whatsoever existed at the time, in the sense that if anybody had asked at that time what the rulings of the divine law are, we would have mentioned among them that pilgrimage is mandatory for the capable person, regardless of whether or not in fact there existed among the Muslims any capable person. But [in the other sense] after this or that person becomes capable, the mandatoriness becomes established in the individual case.

On this basis we realize that for the ruling [that pilgrimage by the capable is mandatory] to be established in the divine law and to be laid down as a divine-law ruling depends only on its having been legislated and promulgated by God Most High, no matter whether or not there is in fact adequate provision [for the act] among the Muslims.

As for the establishment of the mandatoriness of the pilgrimage for this or that legal agent, in addition to God's legislating and promulgation, it depends on the fulfillment of special conditions of capability in the legal agent. The first establishment of the ruling, namely its establishment in the divine law, is called **promulgation**, "the promulgation of the ruling." The second establishment of the ruling, namely its establishment for this or that specific legal agent is called

actuality, the actuality of the ruling or "that which has been promulgated." The promulgation of a ruling means its enactment as law by God. The actuality of a ruling means its being established as a fact for this or that legal agent.

The Subject of a Ruling. The subject of a ruling is a technical term in jurisprudence by which we mean all the things upon which the actuality of the promulgated ruling depends, in the sense of actuality which we have already explained. In the example of the mandatory nature of the pilgrimage, the existence of a capable legal agent is a subject of this [ruling of] mandatoriness, because the actuality of this mandatoriness is dependent upon the existence of a capable legal agent.

Another example: the divine law has ruled that fasting is mandatory for every legal agent who is not traveling and not ill when the new moon of the month of Ramaḍān appears. The first establishment of this ruling depends on its having been promulgated as divine law. Its second establishment, that is to say its actuality, depends on the existence of its subject, namely the existence of a legal agent not traveling and not ill when the new moon of Ramaḍān appears. Thus, a legal agent plus non-travel plus non-illness plus the appearance of the new moon of the month of Ramaḍān are the elements which constitute the complete subject of the ruling that fasting is mandatory. Once we understand the meaning of "the subject of the ruling," we are able to appreciate that the [rational] connection between a ruling and its subject in some respects resembles the connection between an effect and its cause, as with heat and fire. Just as an effect is conditional on its cause, so a ruling is conditional on its subject, because it derives its actuality from the existence of the subject. This is the meaning of the jurisprudential maxim, "The actuality of a ruling is conditional on the actuality of its subject." In other words, the existence of a ruling in actuality is conditional on the existence of its subject in actuality. By virtue of this connection between ruling and subject, a ruling is subsequent in logical order to its subject, just as an effect is subsequent in logical order to its cause.

In the discipline of jurisprudence there are propositions derived from this ruling-subject connection, which appropriately belong among the shared elements in the procedures of derivation.

One such proposition is that it is impossible for the subject of a ruling to be a matter caused by the ruling itself. An example of this is knowledge of the ruling. Knowledge of the ruling is caused by the ruling, since knowledge of something is a derivative of the thing known. It is therefore impossible for knowledge of a ruling to be the subject of the same ruling, as if the Lawgiver should say, "I rule by this ruling [about some matter which is incumbent] upon those who know that this ruling applies to them." That would lead to a vicious circle.

Connections Between a Ruling and its Dependent Object

We have come to understand that a ruling about the mandatory nature of the fast, for example, has a subject composed of a number of elements upon which the actuality of the ruling of mandatoriness depends. The ruling of mandatoriness is not actual and applicable unless there exists a legal agent not traveling and not ill, the new moon of the month of Ramaḍān having appeared. As for the dependent object of this ruling of obligation, it is the action which the legal agent carries out as a result of the ruling of mandatoriness being addressed to him or her: in this example, fasting.

In this light we can distinguish between the dependent object of the ruling of mandatoriness and its subject, for the dependent object exists by reason of the ruling of mandatoriness. The legal agent fasts only because the ruling of mandatoriness of fasting is incumbent upon him or her, whereas the ruling itself exists by reason of its subject. The fasting actually happens only when there exists a legal agent not ill and not traveling and the new moon appears. So we find that the existence of the ruling is conditional on the [prior] existence of its subject, whereas it is a cause of bringing its dependent object into existence and directing the legal agent to it.

On this basis we understand that it is impossible for a ruling of mandatoriness to be a summons to bring into existence its own subject or an incentive toward it for the legal agent in the way that a ruling of mandatoriness summons [a legal agent] to bring the dependent object into existence. The ruling that fasting is mandatory for every legal agent who is not traveling cannot prescribe that the legal agent is not to travel. It prescribes only that one fast if not traveling. The ruling that the pilgrimage is mandatory for every capable person cannot prescribe to a legal agent that he or she must earn a good living so as to come to possess such capability; it only prescribes the pilgrimage for those already capable, because the ruling itself only comes into being after its subject exists. Prior to the existence of its subject, the ruling has no [actual] existence to make it be a summons to bring its own subject into existence. Accordingly, the principle is laid down in the discipline of jurisprudence that "No ruling can be an incentive toward any of the elements internal to the creation of its own subject. Rather, its influence and motivating power are confined to the sphere of its dependent object."

Connections Arising Between a Ruling and its Necessary Preliminaries

The necessary preliminaries upon which the existence of a ruling of "mandatory" depends are of two kinds:

1. Necessary preliminaries upon which the existence of the dependent object depends, such as the travel upon which the performance of the pilgrimage depends, or the ablution upon which prayer depends, or armament upon which the struggle for Islam depends.
2. Necessary preliminaries which enter into the creation of the subject of the ruling of "mandatory," such as the **intention** [of a traveler] to stay [at least ten days in one place], upon which the fast of the month of Ramaḍān depends, or the capability upon which the Islamic pilgrimage depends.

The distinction between these two kinds is that a necessary preliminary that enters into the creation of the subject of the ruling conditions the existence of the ruling of mandatoriness itself. This is so, as we explained earlier, because the existence of a divine-law ruling is conditional upon the existence of its subject. Thus the ruling is conditional upon every necessary preliminary intrinsic to the realization of its subject and cannot exist without it. This is in contrast to necessary preliminaries which do not enter into the creation of the subject and upon which only the existence of the dependent object is conditional. The ruling exists before such necessary preliminaries [need] exist, because they are not included in the subject of the ruling.

Let us explain this matter in terms of the examples of capability and ablution. Capability is a necessary preliminary upon which the Islamic pilgrimage is conditional, and earning the means is a necessary preliminary to this capability, and going to one's shop in the market is a preliminary to earning the means. Since capability enters into the creation of the subject of the ruling that pilgrimage is mandatory, accordingly there is no obligation for the pilgrimage before capability exists, and before those matters upon which capability is conditional exist.

As for ablution, it does not enter into the creation of the subject of the ruling that prayer is mandatory, because the obligation to pray does not anticipate that one will perform ablution in order to direct oneself to the mandatoriness of prayer. On the contrary, one will have already directed oneself to that. It is the dependent object of the obligation [*sc.* to pray] that is conditional on ablution. Ablution is conditional on preparing a sufficient quantity of water, and preparing a sufficient quantity of water is conditional, for example, on opening the storage tank.

There are, then, two series of necessary preliminaries:

1. The first is the series of necessary preliminaries of the dependent object such as the ablution upon which prayer is conditional, and the preparing of water, upon which ablution is conditional, and the opening of the storage tank upon which the preparing of the water is conditional.
2. The second is the series of necessary preliminaries for the obligation itself, such as the capability that is intrinsic to the creation

of the subject of the obligation of the pilgrimage, and acquiring the means upon which the capability is dependent, and the going to one's place in the market upon which acquiring the means is conditional.

The position of the ruling of mandatoriness in respect of this second series and all the necessary preliminaries it contains is always negative, because the existence of the subject of the ruling depends upon these kinds of necessary preliminaries. We have previously recognized that a ruling of mandatoriness cannot be a summons to [create] its own subject. Every necessary preliminary of this kind is called a "preliminary of mandatoriness," or "mandatoriness-related preliminary."

As for the first series and the necessary preliminaries contained in it, the legal agent is responsible for bringing the necessary preliminaries to realization; that is, a person **enjoined** to prayer, for example, is responsible for performing ablution in order to pray. Similarly, a person enjoined to make the pilgrimage is responsible for traveling in order to perform the pilgrimage, and a person enjoined to struggle for Islam is responsible for arming himself or herself in order to struggle.

A point which specialists in jurisprudence have studied is the classification of this responsibility. They have offered two interpretations of it:

1. Some hold that what is legally mandatory upon the enjoined person is prayer and nothing more, excluding the necessary preliminaries of prayer like ablution and the necessary preliminaries to ablution. The person enjoined finds himself rationally [as opposed to legally] responsible for accomplishing ablution and the other preliminaries, because he sees that compliance with the divine-law ruling of mandatoriness is not attainable except by effecting those necessary preliminaries.
2. Others hold that ablution is legally mandatory because it is a preliminary to something [else which is indisputably legally] mandatory, that the preliminary of a mandatory thing is itself legally mandatory. So in a case like this there are two divine-law

> rulings of mandatoriness incumbent upon the legal agent, one being prayer, the other being ablution *quâ* necessary preliminary to prayer. The first is called "mandatory *per se*," being mandatory in its own right. The second is "mandatory *per alienum*," being mandatory for the sake of something else, *i.e.*, for the sake of something else to which it is a necessary preliminary, namely prayer.

The latter explanation has been adopted by a group of specialists in jurisprudence in their belief that there is a connection of necessary concomitance between a thing being mandatory and its necessary preliminaries being mandatory. Whenever [so they say] the Lawgiver makes a ruling about something being mandatory, a ruling is made immediately afterwards whereby its necessary preliminaries are mandatory.

One can object that the ruling of the Lawgiver about the mandatoriness of a necessary preliminary in such a case is otiose and unnecessary, because, if the Lawgiver wished by such a ruling to require the legal agent [to perform] the necessary preliminary, this is already achieved without any need for His ruling about its mandatoriness, since, after the act which is conditional upon the necessary preliminary has been made mandatory, reason comprehends the responsibility of the legal agent in this respect.

If the Lawgiver had some other end in view which moved Him to rule the necessary preliminary mandatory, we have no inkling of it. On that basis, the ruling of the Lawgiver about the mandatoriness of the necessary preliminary would be a nonsense and impossible to establish, let alone necessary to establish, as the proponent of a necessary consequence between [a ruling about] the mandatoriness of a thing and [a ruling about] the mandatoriness of its necessary preliminary would have it.

Connections Within A Single Ruling

Mandatoriness may be connected with one single thing, as with the mandatoriness of prostration for anyone who hears one of the verses of prostration. But mandatoriness may also be connected with a procedure which consists of parts and includes a variety of acts, as with the mandatoriness of prayer, for prayer is a procedure which is composed of parts and includes numerous acts, such as reciting and prostrating and bending and standing upright and uttering the profession of faith and the like. In such a case the procedure in its character as a composite of these parts is mandatory, and every part is mandatory also. The term "independent mandatoriness" is applied to the composite. The term "incorporated mandatoriness" is applied to every part of it, because the mandatoriness attaches to the part in its character as a part incorporated in the composite, not independently of the rest of the parts. The mandatory nature of the part is not an independent ruling but a part of the mandatoriness which is connected with the composite procedure.

For this reason the mandatoriness of every part of prayer, for example, was linked to the mandatoriness of the other parts, because the incorporated mandatorinesses of the parts of the prayer together form a single independent obligation. As a result of that there arises a [rational] connection of concomitance within the framework of a single ruling among the incorporated mandatorinesses in it. The connection of concomitance means that one can neither divide these obligations into parts nor make any separation between them. On the contrary, if any one of them is omitted, omission of the remainder necessarily follows as a result of that [rational] connection of concomitance obtaining between them.

If, for example, ablution is mandatory for a person – and ablution is composed of numerous parts such as washing the face, washing the right hand, washing the left hand, wiping clean the head, and wiping clean the two feet – then an incorporated obligation attaches to each one of these parts in its character as a part of the obligatory ablution. In this case if it is impossible to wash the face because of some illness and on that account the incorporated obligation attaching to washing the face becomes void, it necessarily follows that the obligation of washing the other parts of the body becomes void as well.

No obligation remains to wash the hands alone, as long as one has been unable to wash the face, because these obligations must be looked at as one obligation connected with the entire process, *i.e.*, the ablution. Either the mandatoriness lapses in full or else it applies in full: there is no scope for splitting it into parts.

In this light we perceive the difference between (1) what [happens] when ablution is mandatory through one independent obligation and yet [there remains] the mandatoriness of private prayer through another independent obligation even though there is an impediment to ablution, and (2) what [happens] when ablution is mandatory but there is an impediment to part of it such as washing the face, for example.

In the first case the dispensation from ablution only leads to the lapse of the obligation that was connected with it [and affects nothing else]. In the case of the mandatoriness of private prayer, that obligation remains because it is an independent obligation not tied to the obligation of ablution.

In the second case, when one is dispensed from washing the face and the incorporated mandatoriness of doing so lapses, this [dispensation] leads to lapsing of the mandatoriness of ablution [altogether] and to the elimination of the rest of the incorporated obligations.

You may object: "We understand that a person is enjoined to pray the liturgical prayer and when he becomes mute and is unable to do the recitation in it, he is enjoined to pray without recitation. What is this, except separation between incorporated obligations, and a breech of the connection of concomitance between them?"

The answer is that the mandatoriness of prayer without recitation for a mute person is not a division into parts of the mandatoriness of the complete liturgical prayer. It is another obligation altogether with a different divine articulation [enjoining it], an obligation that was connected with silent prayer from the beginning. The mandatoriness of the complete liturgical prayer (with the corresponding articulation by God) has ceased to apply as a result of the dispensation from recitation. Another [ruling of] mandatoriness deriving from a different divine articulation has replaced it.

3

Procedural Principles

Introduction

In [discussing] the first type [of divine-law argument] we have surveyed the commonly shared jurisprudential elements for derivation that have to do with substantiating arguments. We have studied the types and characteristics of substantiating arguments and distinguished between those in which there is evidence and the other sort.

We intend now to study the commonly shared elements in another situation that arises in derivation, that in which the jurist has failed to attain a substantiating argument which indicates a divine-law ruling, the ruling [proper] remaining unascertainable. In this situation, investigation turns toward an attempt to determine a practical position vis-à-vis that unascertainable ruling as a substitute for the discovery of the ruling itself.

An example of this is the situation of the jurist as regards smoking. At the outset, we suppose that smoking is probably forbidden by the divine law. We begin by directing ourselves to an attempt to obtain a substantiating argument which would specify the divine-law ruling to that effect. As we do not find such an argument, we wonder what the practical position is which we ought to adopt in the face of the unascertainable ruling. Is it necessary for us, first of all, to exercise precaution?

Such is the basic question which the jurist treats in this situation. He or she answers it in the light of certain procedural principles in their quality as commonly shared elements in the procedure of derivation. These principles are the topic of our study at present.

1. The Fundamental Procedural Principle [Precaution]

In order to appreciate the basic procedural principle in the light of which we answer the question of whether **precaution** is necessary in the face of the unknown ruling, we must recur to the starting point which obedience to the Lawgiver imposes on us. We must see whether this starting point imposes upon us precaution in the situation of doubt and lack of an argument for the prohibition [of smoking] or not. In order to recur to the starting point which obedience to the Master, praised be He, imposes on us, we must determine that starting point. What is the starting point that obedience to the Lawgiver imposes on us and that it is mandatory for us to consult concerning our position?

The answer is that this starting point is reason, because a human being understands through reason that God, praised be He, has a rightful claim to the obedience of His servants. On the basis of this rightful claim to obedience reason decrees that obedience to the Lawgiver is mandatory for the human being in order that he or she fulfill His rightful claim. We, then, obey God Most High and submit to divine-law rulings, because reason imposes that upon us, not because the Lawgiver ordered us to obey Him. Otherwise the question would be set for us yet again, why do we obey the order of the Lawgiver to us to obey the order of the Lawgiver? What is the starting point which imposes obedience to Him upon us? And so forth, until we reach reason's judgment that obedience is mandatory, a judgment resting upon the basis of that which reason grasps concerning God's right to claim obedience from humankind.

If reason is what imposes obedience to the Lawgiver on the basis of its grasp of His rightful claim to obedience, then it is mandatory to have recourse to reason in determining the answer to the question posed.

In this case we ought to study the rightful claim to obedience which reason grasps, and also the limits [of that claim]. Is the rightful claim of All-Praiseworthy God restricted to the realm of *known* injunctions alone, in the sense that All-Praiseworthy God has a rightful claim to obedience from man only in respect of those injunctions which man knows about? [If so,] a rightful claim to obedience would not extend to injunctions about which there is doubt and of which man possesses no knowledge.

Or is it rather the case that the rightful claim to obedience, as reason understands it in the sphere of known injunctions, is also understood by reason in the realm of *possible* injunctions, in the sense that it is part of the rightful claim of God on people that they obey Him in both known and possible injunctions? In that case, if a person knows of an injunction, then is it not part of God's rightful claim that s/he obey Him? – and if s/he conceives of an obligation as possible, is it not part of God's rightful claim that s/he exercise precaution, and thus renounce anything which may possibly be prohibited, and perform anything which may possibly be mandatory?

The correct view in our opinion is that the **source of law** in the case of every injunction that is possible [but not definitely known] is precaution, as a result of the inclusion of possible injunctions in the rightful claim to obedience. For reason understands that the Master has a rightful claim of obedience from human beings not in known injunctions alone, but in possible injunctions as well, as long as it has not been established by a [substantiating] argument that the Master is not concerned with a possible injunction to such a degree as to call for requiring the legal agent to exercise precaution.

This means that in a fundamental way whenever we consider prohibition or mandatoriness possible, the source of law is the exercise of precaution. Thus we omit what we consider to be possibly prohibited and perform what we consider to be possibly mandatory. We do not depart from this source of law except when it is established by [substantiating] argument that the Lawgiver is not concerned with a possible injunction to such a degree as to impose precaution and is, in fact, satisfied with the abandonment of precaution. At that point the legal agent ceases to be responsible for [complying with] the possible injunction.

Therefore precaution is mandatory according to reason on occasions of doubt. This mandatoriness is called the priority of precaution or the priority of **engagement**, *i.e.*, the engagement of human responsibility with a possible injunction. We set aside this principle [only] when we know that the Lawgiver is satisfied with the abandonment of precaution.

Hence the priority of precaution is the basic procedural principle.

Many specialists in jurisprudence disagree with that point of view due to a belief that the default assumption about a legal agent should be that he or she is not responsible for injunctions about which there is [any] doubt [at all], even if their importance were supposed to be highly probable.

These leading figures believe that it is reason which rules for denying such responsibility, because it understands that it would be wrong for the Master to punish a legal agent for acting contrary to an injunction which has not been conveyed to him or her. For this reason the term applied to this source of law from their point of view is "The principle of the wrongness of punishment without clear [divine] statement" or "rational exemption," which is to say that reason judges that for the Master to punish a legal agent for rejecting the obligation subject to doubt would be wrong. As long as the legal agent is immune from punishment, he or she is not responsible and precaution is not mandatory for him or her. In this connection, they offer as evidence the conduct of rational people, which presumes the non-condemnation by masters of persons under injunction in situations of doubt and the failure to establish a [divine-law] argument.

Such behavior indicates that in the opinion of rational people punishment is wrong without a **clear statement** [of the pertinent injunction].

To grasp whether reason does or does not judge in favor of the wrongness of God Most High punishing a legal agent for rejecting an injunction subject to doubt, it is necessary to know the limits of that rightful claim to obedience which belongs to God Most High. If this rightful claim includes injunctions subject to doubt that the legal agent supposes to be of great importance, then, as we have come to understand, God's punishment of the legal agent if he or she acts contrary to them is not wrong, because by rejection he or she falls short of observing the rightful claim of his/her Lord and Master and so deserves punishment. The evidence offered about the behavior of rational people has no bearing on the case, because it establishes only that a rightful claim to obedience to the customary sort of masters specifically applies to [undoubtedly] known obligations [alone]. This [line of reasoning] does not require that obedience to God Most High work that way as well. What is there, then, to prevent us from separating the two sorts of rightful claim and not making one of them necessarily broader than the other? [Why, nothing at all! We are indeed to assume that God has broader claims than human masters.]

The primary [procedural] principle, then, is the priority of precaution.

2. The Secondary Procedural Principle

The basic procedural principle has been inverted by a ruling of the Lawgiver into a secondary procedural principle, the priority of exemption which advocates the non-mandatoriness of precaution.

The cause of this inversion is that we know by way of a clear divine-law proclamation that the Lawgiver is not concerned with possible injunctions to the degree that precaution is required of the legal agent. Rather, He is satisfied with the abandonment of precaution.

The argument for this inversion is to be found in numerous divine-law prooftexts. One of the most famous of these is the prophetic prooftext [a hadith from Muhammad] "My religious community are relieved of that which they do not know." [The priority of exemption] can even be inferred from some verses of the Qur'ān, as when God Most High says "We do not punish until [after] We send a Messenger" (*Banī 'Isrā'īl* XVII: 15). "Messenger" is understood to imply a clear statement and a [substantiating] argument. The verse shows that there is no punishment without an argument. In this way the [effective] procedural principle becomes that precaution is not mandatory rather than mandatory, taking the point of departure to be exemption based on divine law rather than engagement [*i.e.*, precaution] based on reason.

This secondary procedural principle includes occasions of doubt concerning mandatoriness, and, equally, occasions of doubt concerning prohibition, because the prophetic text cited is absolute [and without any restriction to positive commands]. Doubt concerning mandatoriness is called "uncertainty concerning the mandatory" and doubt about prohibition is called "uncertainty concerning the prohibited." The principle [of exemption] also covers doubt, whatever its cause. On this account we adhere to exemption when we are in doubt concerning an injunction, regardless of whether our doubt has arisen from an absence of clarity concerning whether the Lawgiver ever promulgated the injunction in the first place, or from absence of knowledge as to whether or not its subject has been realized. An example of the first is when we have become doubtful concerning the mandatoriness of the prayer for the Feast [*i.e.*, the Feast of Sacrifice or the feast at the end of the Ramaḍān fast] or concerning the prohibitedness of smoking; this is called "uncertainty concerning the ruling."

An example of the second case is when we have become uncertain concerning the mandatoriness of the pilgrimage because of lack of knowledge as to the sufficiency of ability [to perform it] even though we know that the Lawgiver promulgated the mandatoriness of pilgrimage for the capable person. [This is called "uncertainty concerning the subject of the ruling."] If you wish, you may say that the legal agent in the case of "uncertainty concerning the ruling" doubts about [the original existence of] the promulgation, whereas in the case of doubt about the subject of a ruling he or she doubts about [the current existence of] what was promulgated. Each of these cases is an occasion to which exemption applies on the basis of divine law.

3. The Principle of the Inculpatoriness of Non-specific Knowledge

You may know that your elder brother has traveled to Mecca. You may be in doubt about his travel, but, nevertheless you know that one of your brothers, the elder or the younger, has in fact traveled to Mecca. And you may be in doubt about their traveling together, and not know whether one of them [in particular] traveled to Mecca or not.

Of these three cases, the first one is called **detailed knowledge**, because in the first case you know that your elder brother traveled to Mecca, and no hesitation or uncertainty faces you. Hence this kind of knowledge is detailed. To the second case the name **non-specific knowledge** is applied, because in this case you find two elements paired: the first is an element of clarity and the other is an element of hiddenness. The element of clarity is represented in your knowledge that one of your two brothers has in fact traveled, and you are in no doubt about this truth. The element of hiddenness and obscurity is represented in your doubt and your hesitation to specify which brother. Accordingly this is called a case of non-specific knowledge. It [actually] is [some sort of] knowledge, because you have no doubt concerning the travel of one of your brothers. Yet there is non-specificity and doubt, because you do not know which of your brothers has traveled.

Each of them, the journey of the elder brother and the journey of the younger brother, is called an alternative of the non-specific knowledge in question, because you know that one of the two – but there is no way to specify which – has actually traveled.

The best lexical pattern to represent the structure of non-specific knowledge – its mental containing of two [alternative] elements – is "either ... or," since in the preceding example you would say "Either my elder brother or my younger brother traveled." In this lexical pattern, the aspect of asserting the existence of something corresponds to the element of clarity and knowledge, while the aspect of hesitation which the word "either" conceptualizes corresponds to the element of hiddenness and doubt. Whenever it is possible to use a lexical pattern of this type the existence of non-specific knowledge in our minds is indicated.

The name "elementary" or "primary" or "simple doubt" is applied to the third case. It is pure doubt unmixed with any tinge of knowledge. It is called "elementary" or "primary" doubt to distinguish it from doubt as to which alternative of non-specific knowledge is true, because doubt concerning one alternative of non-specific knowledge exists as a result of the knowledge itself [and so is to be called secondary rather than primary]. Thus you are in doubt as to whether the traveler is your elder brother or younger brother as a result of your knowledge that one of the two without specification undoubtedly has traveled. Doubt in the third case exists in a primary way without any prior knowledge.

All three situations may exist in our minds vis-à-vis a divine-law ruling. (1) The obligation of the morning liturgical prayer is known in all its details. (2) The midday liturgical prayer on Friday is in doubt, a doubt which arises from the non-specific knowledge of the mandatoriness either of the midday liturgical prayer or of the Friday liturgical prayer on that day. (3) The mandatoriness of the liturgical prayer of the Major Feast is the subject of **primary doubt** not joined to any non-specific knowledge. These are all examples of uncertainty concerning a divine-law ruling.

It is possible to find the same kinds of examples for uncertainty concerning the subject of a ruling. (1) You may know on one occasion in exact detail about the dripping of a drop of blood into a certain vessel [which makes the contents of the vessel impure]. (2) On another occasion you may know in a non-specific way of its dripping into one of two vessels. (3) In a third case you may be in doubt in a primary way about the basic fact of any blood dripping at all.

In our discussion of the secondary procedural principle [exemption] which inverted the basic procedural principle [precaution] we were talking about the third situation, that is, the case of primary doubt not connected with non-specific knowledge.

Now we will study the situation of doubt arising from non-specific knowledge, that is, doubt in the second case of the three cases mentioned above. This means that we have [up to now] studied doubt in its simple form. We will now study it after we have added a new element to it, which is non-specific knowledge. Does the secondary procedural principle [of exemption] apply to it as it applied to cases of primary doubt or not?

THE INCULPATORINESS OF NON-SPECIFIC KNOWLEDGE

In the light of what has preceded we are able to analyze non-specific knowledge into (1) knowledge about one or the other of two things, and (2) doubt concerning each thing taken separately. So on Friday we know the mandatoriness of one of two things, the liturgical midday prayer or the liturgical Friday prayer, and we have doubts about the mandatoriness of the midday liturgical prayer just as we doubt the mandatoriness of the Friday prayer. Knowledge of the mandatoriness of one of the two matters – in its quality as knowledge – is included in the principle of the probativity of assurance which we have studied above. On that account reason does not permit us to omit the two matters together – the midday and Friday liturgical prayers – because were we to abandon them both, we would go against our knowledge that one of the two is mandatory, and knowledge is evidence according to reason in all cases whether it be specific or non-specific.

The predominant jurisprudential view in respect to non-specific knowledge believes not only in the established nature of the probativity of knowledge about one of two [alternative] things but also in the impossibility of removing this probativity from non-specific knowledge, and the impossibility of the Lawgiver's granting permission to reject such knowledge by abandoning both alike, just as it is impossible for the Lawgiver to remove from detailed knowledge its probativity and to give permission to reject detailed knowledge. All of this is in accordance with the preceding discussion of assurance and how it is impossible that deterrence from acting according to assurance should come from the Lawgiver.

As for each of the two alternatives of non-specific knowledge, that is, the mandatoriness of the liturgical prayer by itself and the mandatoriness of the Friday prayer by itself, it is an injunction subject to doubt and not known.

It might appear at first sight that the secondary procedural principle – that is, the priority of exemption – which rejects precaution in the case of doubtful injunctions, could apply, because each of the two alternatives is an injunction subject to doubt.

However, the predominant view in jurisprudence upholds the impossibility of the secondary procedural principle applying to an alternative of non-specific knowledge. The argument for this assertion is that application of exemption to both alternatives together would lead to exemption from responsibility for the midday liturgical prayer and the Friday liturgical prayer and [it would lead to] permission to abandon both of them alike. This latter conclusion is in opposition to the probativity of assurance concerning the mandatoriness of one of the two matters, because the probativity of assurance imposes on us that we perform one of the two at very least. Had the Lawgiver ruled for exemption from both of the alternatives, the meaning of that would be His granting permission to act contrary to one's knowledge, which, as shown previously, is impossible.

Moreover, applying the principle of exemption to one of the alternatives and not the other, although it would not lead to giving permission to abandon both matters together, nevertheless is also impossible, because we would then wonder which of the two alternatives to assume that the principle applies to and which to prefer over the other. We will come to know that we do not possess any justification for preferring either alternative over the other, because the relation of the principle to both is the same.

Thus there results from this line of inference the opinion that the secondary procedural principle of the priority of exemption does not apply to either one of the two alternatives. This means that each of the alternatives of non-specific knowledge continues to be included within the scope of the basic procedural principle which advocates precaution inasmuch as the secondary principle cannot apply [to such knowledge]. On this basis we understand the difference between primary doubt, and doubt deriving from non-specific knowledge. The former falls within the scope of the secondary principle, which is exemption, and the latter falls within the scope of the primary principle, which is the priority of precaution.

In light of that we recognize that what is mandatory for us according to reason on occasions of non-specific knowledge is the performance of both alternatives, that is to say, the midday liturgical prayer and the Friday prayer in the preceding example, because both of them fall within the scope of the priority of precaution. Jurisprudence gives the name "assured compliance" to the performance of both aspects together, because the legal agent on performing them together is assured that he or she has complied with the injunction of the Master, just as the name "assured non-compliance" is applied to the abandonment of the two aspects together. As for obeying one of the two and abandoning the other, the terms "possible compliance" and "possible non-compliance" are applied to the two [both to the obeying and to the abandoning] because the legal agent in this situation may possibly have complied with the Master's injunction, but also may possibly have gone against it.

THE ANALYTICAL RESOLUTION OF NON-SPECIFIC KNOWLEDGE

If you find two glasses of water one or both of which may be impure, but in any case you know that they are not both **pure**, there arises in your mind non-specific knowledge of the impure nature of one of the two glasses, no telling which. If later on it happens that you discover the impure nature of one of the two glasses and you know that one particular glass is impure, your non-specific knowledge will cease to exist because of this detailed knowledge, because now, after your discovery of the impure nature of that particular glass, you will not know in a non-specific way about the impure nature of one of the glasses, no telling which. Rather you will know in a detailed way about the impure nature of one glass but be in [primary or total] doubt about the impurity of the other. Therefore you cannot use the lexical pattern "either … or" which expresses non-specific knowledge, and so you cannot say "Either this one is impure or that one is." Rather, one is definitely unclean and you simply don't know about the other.

In jurisprudential usage this is expressed as "analytic resolution of non-specific knowledge into detailed knowledge of one of the alternatives and primary doubt concerning the other." In this case the impurity of one particular glass has become known in detail, and the impurity of the other glass has become doubtful in a primary way after non-specific knowledge ceased. Detailed knowledge [about one glass] then has its [usual] consequences of probativity, while the primary doubt [about the other glass] is handled by taking exemption as the point of departure, exemption being the secondary procedural principle which applies on all occasions of primary doubt.

OCCASIONS OF HESITATION

We have come to know that the secondary procedural principle of the priority of exemption decides about doubt when the doubt is primary.

But when doubt is combined with non-specific knowledge, the primary procedural principle [of precaution] decides.

Sometimes the kind of doubt may be concealed and one does not know whether it is primary doubt or doubt combined with non-specific knowledge, or, to express it in another way, doubt deriving from non-specific knowledge. An example of this variety of doubt is the problem of the "alternation of a matter between the minimum and the maximum," as it is called by the specialists in jurisprudence. It is the problem faced when mandatoriness according to the divine law is associated with a procedure composed of parts, like the liturgical prayer. We know that the procedure includes nine specific parts but we are in doubt about the inclusion in it of a tenth part, and no [substantiating] argument exists which would confirm or deny its inclusion. In this case the jurist tries to define the practical position and wonders whether precaution is mandatory for the legal agent. So does s/he perform nine parts and add to them this tenth, the inclusion of which may possibly be mandatory, in order to carry out what is mandatory according to any estimate [of its extent]? Or is performing the nine parts, the mandatoriness of which is known, sufficient, with the tenth part, the mandatoriness of which is not known, not being demanded?

Specialists in jurisprudence have two different answers to this question, each of which represents a certain orientation in interpreting the position. One of the two orientations advocates the mandatoriness of precaution in conformity with the primary procedural principle, because doubt concerning the tenth part is joined with non-specific knowledge. This non-specific knowledge is the knowledge by a legal agent that the Lawgiver has made some composite of parts mandatory but does not know whether it is a composite of nine or of ten parts, those known plus one extra.

The other orientation applies the secondary procedural principle [exemption] to the doubt concerning the mandatoriness of the tenth part by virtue of it being primary doubt not connected with non-specific knowledge. They say this is so because that non-specific knowledge which the supporters of the first orientation assert to be present is analytically resolved into detailed knowledge, which is the knowledge by the legal agent that the nine parts are mandatory in any case, because they are mandatory regardless of whether they are accompanied by the tenth part or not. So this detailed knowledge leads to the analytical resolution of that non-specific knowledge. It is for this reason that we are not able to use the lexical pattern which expresses non-specific knowledge [*i.e.* "either ... or"]. So it is not possible to claim that we know "Either the nine parts are mandatory, or the ten." Rather, we know the mandatoriness of the nine parts in any case, but we are in doubt about the mandatoriness of the tenth. Thus doubt concerning the tenth becomes primary doubt after analytical resolution of non-specific knowledge, and the principle of exemption is in effect.

The sound view is the [second] opinion which favors exemption for the parts not known, concerning the inclusion of which within the scope of what is mandatory there is doubt.

4. The Presumption of Continuity

In the light of the preceding we know that the principle of exemption is effective on occasions of primary uncertainty excluding uncertainty associated with non-specific knowledge.

There exists another source of law similar to exemption, and it is what the specialists in jurisprudence call the **presumption of continuity**. The meaning of the presumption of continuity is the ruling of the Lawgiver that the legal agent should maintain adherence in practice to anything about which he or she was formerly certain but then subsequently has come to doubt that it persists. An example is when we are certain that water is intrinsically pure, but if then something which has become impure through contact with something intrinsically unclean strikes the water, we have doubt about the persistence of the purity of the water because we do not know whether or not the water would become impure by contact.

The presumption of continuity gives the legal agent its judgment in favor of maintaining adherence in practice to the same preceding condition of which he or she had certainty. In the preceding example, the preceding condition was the purity of the water. The meaning of maintaining adherence in practice to the preceding condition is to apply the effects of the preceding situation from a practical standpoint. So if the preceding situation was one of purity, we deal in our actions as if that purity continues. If the previous state was one of mandatoriness, we deal in our actions as if the mandatoriness continues, and so forth. The [substantiating] argument for the presumption of continuity is the statement of Imam Ja'far aṣ-Ṣādiq which is related in the reliable account of Zurārah, "Certainty cannot be destroyed by doubt."

We conclude from that statement that any case of primary doubt in which the certainty of something is at first available, and doubt about its persistence only comes in afterwards, the presumption of continuity applies and takes effect.

THE PREVIOUS CONDITION OF CERTAINTY

We have come to understand that a previous state of certainty is a basic condition for the presumption of continuity to have effect. The previous state may sometimes be (1) a general ruling concerning which we know that it was promulgated by the Lawgiver and was established in the legislative realm, but we do not know the boundaries of this ruling, imposed upon it at the time of its promulgation, and the range of the ruling's extent in the legislative realm. So our uncertainty is related to the ruling and the presumption of continuity applies to the ruling itself, as with the presumption of continuity of the persistence of the water's purity after being struck by something extrinsically impure. One speaks of "the presumption of continuity in respect of the ruling."

Sometimes the previous condition may be (2) something from the physical world of things [hence subject to change and decay] about which we know its previous existence but we do not know of its persistence, and moreover it is the subject of a divine-law ruling. So the uncertainty is related to the subject. The presumption of continuity applies to the subject of the ruling. Examples of [this case] are (1) the presumption of the continuity of the rectitude of a leader of the liturgical prayer about the fresh occurrence of whose immorality there is doubt, and (2) the presumption of the continuity of the impure state of a garment about which there is doubt concerning the fresh occurrence of its cleaning. This is called "presumption of continuity concerning the subject of a divine-law ruling," because the presumption of continuity pertains to the subject of the ruling. In the first case, [the presumption of continuity] yields permission to follow the prayer leader, and in the second, the impermissibility of the liturgical prayer [while wearing the impure garment].

In the world of jurisprudence there is an orientation that denies the effectiveness of the presumption of continuity concerning uncertainty related to the ruling and applies it exclusively to uncertainty related to the subject. There is no doubt that the presumption of continuity in the case of uncertainty related to the subject is established with certainty from the argument for it, because the reliable report of Zurārah in which the Imam Ja'far aṣ-Ṣādiq granted the presumption of continuity involved an obscurity related to the subject of a ruling, namely doubt about the fresh occurrence of sleep which would vitiate previous ablution. But this fact does not prevent one from adhering to general application of the words of the Imam in his statement "Certainty cannot be destroyed by doubt" so as to establish the generality of the principle for all situations. It is up to one who claims that this principle is only for the case of doubt concerning the subject of a ruling to adduce a context in order to restrict this general application.

DOUBT CONCERNING PERSISTENCE

Doubt concerning persistence is the other basic condition for application of the presumption of continuity. Specialists in jurisprudence subdivide doubt about persistence into two categories according to the nature of the previous situation about the persistence of which we have doubt. They do so because the previous situation may sometimes (1) be susceptible by its nature to extension in time, and we doubt about its persistence only as a result of the possible existence of some external factor which might have led to termination of the previous situation.

An example of that is the purity of water, because the purity of water continues by its nature and extends onward if no external factor interferes. We have doubts about its persistence only because of the entrance of an external factor into the situation, namely the striking of the water by something extrinsically impure. The same is the case with the impurity of a garment, because if the garment becomes impure, its impurity remains and extends onwards as long as a certain external factor does not exist, namely washing. This kind of doubt about the persistence of the previous situation is called "doubt concerning intervention."

Sometimes (2) the previous situation may be incapable of extension in time. Rather, it comes to an end by its nature at a specific time and we have doubt about its persistence as a result of the possibility of its ending by its nature without the entry of any external factor into the situation. An example is the daytime of the month of Ramaḍān, in which fasting is mandatory when a fasting person has doubt about the persistence of daytime. For daytime comes to an end by its nature and it is not possible that it extend onwards in time. So doubt about its persistence is not produced by the possibility of the existence of an external factor. It is the result of the very possibility of the ending of daytime by its own nature and the using up of its capacity and ability to continue. Doubt of this type about the persistence of the preceding situation is called "doubt concerning original capability," because the doubt concerns the extent of the capability of daytime and its tendency to continue. An orientation exists in jurisprudence which rejects the effectiveness of the presumption of continuity if the doubt about the continuity of the previous situation is of this variety of doubt concerning capability, and restricts it to situations of doubt concerning an intervention. The sound view is the non-restrictive understanding, adhering to the general application of the argument of the presumption of continuity.

UNITY OF THE SUBJECT AND THE PRESUMPTION OF CONTINUITY

Specialists in jurisprudence are agreed that one of the conditions of the presumption of continuity is the unity of the subject. By that they mean that the doubt is directed toward the same situation that we formerly occupied in certainty. So the presumption of continuity does not apply if the thing doubted and the thing held in certainty are dissimilar. For example, if we were certain of the impurity of water and then it became steam and we are in doubt about the impurity of this steam, the presumption of continuity would not apply in this situation, because that which we were certain to be unclean was water, and the thing about which we presently have doubts is steam, and steam is not water, so the place from which doubt and certainty have issued is not one and the same.

4

The Conflict of Arguments

In what has preceded we have come to know that arguments are of two kinds: substantiating arguments and procedural principles. From here on the discussion will first turn to the conflict between two arguments of the substantiating sort, then to the conflict between two procedural principles, and thirdly to conflict between a substantiating argument and a procedural principle. So we will speak in what follows in sequence on the three points we have mentioned, God willing.

1. Conflict Between Substantiating Arguments

The meaning of a conflict between two substantiating arguments is the mutual incompatibility of the two things signified by them. There are several cases:

1. In the realm of the verbal divine-law argument, two statements issuing from an infallible person may [seem to] conflict.
2. A verbal divine-law argument may conflict with a rational argument.
3. Two rational arguments may conflict.

THE CASE OF CONFLICT BETWEEN TWO VERBAL ARGUMENTS

In the case of conflict between two verbal [substantiating] arguments certain principles [for resolution] exist, a number of which we will review in what follows.

1. It is impossible that two statements from an infallible person should each reveal in an assured fashion a kind of ruling [*sc.*, one of the five types of injunctive ruling] which disagrees with the ruling that the other statement discloses, since such a conflict between two clear statements would imply that the infallible person fell into self-contradiction, which is impossible.

2. One of the two statements issuing from an infallible person may be a clear and assured prooftext, while the other indicates by its prima-facie sense something which would be incompatible with the clear meaning of the former statement.

For example, the Lawgiver says in a tradition, "When fasting one may immerse oneself in water at the time of one's fast." But in another tradition the Lawgiver says "Do not immerse yourself in water while you are fasting." The first statement signifies clearly the permissibility of the fasting person immersing himself or herself. The second statement contains the prohibitive form of the verb, signifying by its prima-facie sense that the same thing is forbidden, because forbiddenness is the closest of meanings to the prohibitive form, although it can be used figuratively to signify discouragement. So a conflict arises between the first text being clearly for permissibility and the second text being prima-facie for prohibitedness, because permissibility and prohibitedness do not agree. In this situation it is mandatory to adopt the clear assured statement because it leads to knowledge of the divine-law ruling. We explain the second statement in light of the first and take the prohibitive form in it to imply no more than discouragement in order to harmonize it with the clear and assured text signifying permissibility. On this basis the jurist moves forward to derive a general principle, namely that one should adopt an argument for permissibility and **dispensation** when another argument for prohibitedness or mandatoriness based on the prohibitive or imperative verb form conflicts with it, because the linguistic form is not absolutely clear, whereas an argument for permissibility and dispensation is most often [absolutely clear].

3. The subject of a ruling which one of two [conflicting] statements indicates may be narrower in scope and more specific in application than the subject of the ruling which the other statement indicates. For example, it is said in one text "Interest is prohibited", and it is said in another "Interest between father and son is permitted." The prohibitedness that the first text indicates is the general subject [of a ruling for prohibitedness], because with its absolute phrasing it inhibits any usurious transaction with any person. The subject of the [ruling for] permissibility in the second text is specific because it permits interest specifically between father and son. In this case the second text takes precedence over the first, because it is considered in its character as the more specific about a subject than the first, as a context for the first. The argument is that if the speaker had combined the two statements and said "Interest is prohibited in dealing with anybody, but there is nothing wrong with it between father and son," the specific would cancel the effect of the general and the prima-facie presumption of generality.

We have noted previously that a context, whether conjunctive or disjunctive, takes precedence over what it contextualizes.

Giving precedence to the specific over the general is called "specification of the general" when generality is established by one of the verbal markers of generalization, but "**restriction** of the general" when generality is established by absolute expression without any mention of restriction. In the first case the specific is called "the specifying," and in the second case "the restricting." On this basis the jurist follows a general principle in his derivation, namely that one adopts what is specifying or restricting and gives it precedence over what is [explicitly] general or expressed absolutely. Nevertheless, what is general or expressed absolutely is evidence about anything which has not been singled out by specification or restriction, since it is impermissible to abstain from using evidence except insofar as other evidence turns up which is stronger to the contrary, and no further.

4. One statement might be arguing that such-and-such a ruling is established given such-and-such a subject whereas the other rejects that in a specified case by rejecting that subject. For example, it is said in one statement "The pilgrimage is mandatory for a capable person," but in another statement, "A debtor is not a capable person." The first statement makes pilgrimage mandatory assuming a certain defined subject [of the ruling has come to exist], namely a capable person. The second denies the attribute "capable" to a debtor. One goes by the second statement, which is termed **overruling**, while the first statement is "overruled."

The principles which require giving precedence to one argument over another mentioned in (2) and (3) and (4) above are called "common-usage principles of accommodation."

5. When there is no clear, assured statement in either of the conflicting texts, nor anything that makes sense as a context to explain the other, whether as a specification or a restriction or an overruling, then one may not use either of the two conflicting arguments because both are on a par and there is no basis on which to prefer one to the other.

OTHER SITUATIONS OF CONFLICT

Situations of conflict between a verbal argument and an argument of another kind or between two arguments which are not verbal arguments also have principles [of resolution] which we will indicate in the following sections.

1. An assured rational argument cannot conflict with an assured verbal argument, because if an argument of that sort were to conflict with a clear prooftext from an infallible person, that would lead to calling the infallible person untruthful or calling him mistaken – which is impossible.

Scholars of the divine law therefore say that there cannot be any conflict between clear divine-law prooftexts and assured arguments of reason. Not only does **dogmatic belief** propound this truth, it is demonstrated by induction based on the divine-law prooftexts and by study of the assured data of the Qur'ān and the sunna, for they altogether agree with reason. There is nothing whatsoever in them that conflicts with the assured dictates of reason.

2. When there is a conflict between a verbal argument and another type of argument which is not assured, we give precedence to the verbal argument, because it is evidence. As for the non-verbal argument, it is not evidence, seeing that it does not lead to assurance.

3. When an unclear verbal argument conflicts with an assured rational argument, the rational argument is given precedence over the verbal, because the rational one leads to knowledge of the divine-law ruling. An unclear verbal argument only indicates a prima-facie sense, and, by a ruling of the Lawgiver, the prima-facie sense is evidence about a divine-law ruling only when we do not know anything to the contrary. In the case at hand, however, we know, in light of an assured rational argument, that the infallible person did not intend that a prima-facie meaning should be [drawn] from the verbal argument which would conflict with the argument of reason, so there is no freedom to adopt the prima-facie sense.

4. When two non-verbal arguments conflict, both of them cannot be assured, because that would lead to contradiction. Sometimes one of them is assured to the exclusion of the other, and then the assured argument is adopted.

2. Conflict Between [Procedural] Principles

The outstanding case of conflict between procedural principles is that which exists between exemption and the presumption of continuity. For example, we know that fasting is mandatory from the appearance of the dawn of daytime in the month of Ramaḍān until the setting of the sun, but we are in doubt about the persistence of the obligation after sunset until the disappearance of twilight. In this situation the key elements for the presumption of continuity – first, a previous state of certainty about the mandatoriness and, second, doubt about the persistence of that state – are present. By a ruling based on the presumption of continuity it would be determined that one is bound in practice to [assume] the persistence of the mandatoriness [of fasting].

Yet from another point of view we observe that the situation is included within the scope of exemption as a source of law, because there is primary doubt about an injunction – doubt not linked to non-specific knowledge. Exemption as a source of law rejects the mandatoriness of precaution in practice and would relieve us of the mandatoriness [of fasting during twilight]. So which of the two sources of law do we adopt?

The answer is that we adopt the presumption of continuity and give it precedence over exemption as a source of law. This is agreed upon among the jurists. The predominant opinion among them in justification of this is that the argument from the presumption of continuity overrules the argument from the principle of exemption, because the argument for exemption is a prophetic text [a hadith from Muhammad] which says "What they do not know is removed [as an obligation]," the subject of which ruling is anything that is not known. [That is, whenever anything is not assuredly known, non-mandatoriness is the divine-law ruling established by this prooftext.]

The argument for the presumption of continuity is the prooftext saying "Certainty is never destroyed by doubt." By close examination of the two texts we observe that the argument based on the presumption of continuity does away with doubt and assumes that [the former state of] certainty continues as it was. Thus the subject of exemption as [the appropriate] source of law [namely something that is not known] is removed.

In the example of the mandatoriness of fasting, we cannot rely on the principle of exemption concerning the mandatoriness of the fast after sunset in its character as a doubtful obligation, because the presumption of continuity assumes that this mandatoriness is known, so the argument for the presumption of continuity overrules the argument for exemption, because it refutes [the supposed existence of doubt, which is] the subject of [a ruling for the applicability of] exemption.

3. Conflict Between the Two Types of Argument

We now come to the hypothetical possibility of a conflict between a substantiating argument and a procedural principle such as exemption or the presumption of continuity.

The truth is that when an argument is assured, conflict between it and the procedural principles is rationally inconceivable, because an assured argument for, say, mandatoriness leads to knowledge of the divine-law ruling. Given knowledge of the divine-law ruling, there is no scope for reliance on any procedural principle, because the procedural principles apply only in circumstances of doubt. After all, we have noted above that exemption as a source of law has as its subject anything that is not known and the presumption of continuity has as its subject our being in doubt concerning the persistence of something we used to be certain about. When an argument is assured, the subject of these sources of law or principles [*sc.*, ignorance or doubt or uncertainty] is absent.

Hypothesizing even a hint of conflict between an argument and a procedural principle is possible only if the argument is not assured, as when the **account** of a single reliable person is taken as an argument for mandatoriness or prohibition. As mentioned above, the account of a single reliable person is a **presumptive** argument which the Lawgiver has ruled it mandatory to follow and to accept as an argument. But from another direction, there is the principle of exemption which broadens and permits [instead of mandating or prohibiting.]

Take, for example, the report of a single reliable source indicating the prohibitedness of immersion in water for the person fasting. Such prohibitedness, if we view it from the standpoint of the account, would be a divine-law ruling which the presumptive argument stands upon. But if we view [this prohibitedness] in its quality as an uncertainly known injunction, we would find that the argument [*i.e.*, the prooftext] for exemption "That which is not known is removed" includes this case. Does the jurist in such circumstances define his position on the basis of the presumptive argument [being] respected [as assured], or on the basis of the procedural principle [of exemption]?

Specialists in jurisprudence call the presumptive argument an **indication**, and the term "conflict between indications and procedural principles" is applied to the situation we have been discussing.

There is no doubt about this situation among the scholars of jurisprudence: precedence must be given to the account of the single reliable source and similar authorized arguments over the procedural principles of exemption and the like, because a presumptive argument for the probativity of which the Lawgiver has ruled, by that very ruling of the Lawgiver, fulfills the role of an assured argument. An assured argument denies [the existence of] the subject of the procedural principles [*i.e.*, uncertainty] and leaves no scope for any procedural principle, as does a presumptive proof to which the Lawgiver has assigned the same role and which He has commanded us to accept as an argument. Hence it is frequently said that an indication overrules the procedural principles.

Analytical Summary by the Translator

[All the original headers and subheaders are given, but the numbering of sections and division into four main parts is not in the printed Arabic book. Material that is more commentary than summary appears inside square brackets.]

1. Characterization of Jurisprudence

1. AN INTRODUCTORY WORD

Jurisprudence is the general study of how the jurist derives valid divine-law rulings. Such derivation is a practical necessity for every Muslim, and a discipline concerned with it became necessary as the passage of time made the sources of these rulings more and more obscure. To derive a ruling one must adduce an argument. This may be done either directly (if one of the sources of law unmistakably addresses the issue at hand) or indirectly. In the former case, we speak of a "substantiating argument" or simply "an argument;" in the latter case, of a "procedural argument." (A "substantiating argument" is an argument which obtains a secure grasp of the relevant legal ruling.) The second type is called "procedural" with reference to the jurist's procedure after failing to find a substantiating argument. The discipline of jurisprudence is concerned with the general principles of deploying these arguments, with the elements common to the derivation of many particular valid rulings.

2. CHARACTERIZATION OF THE DISCIPLINE OF JURISPRUDENCE

The author gives three case studies of valid derivation of legal rulings and points out what they have in common, since that is what jurisprudence is concerned with. In all three the source of the ruling is a tradition, although the traditional accounts cited are of course quite different and transmitted by different transmitters. Common to all, though, is a concern with which transmitters are reliable. Similarly, all three cases involve understanding what common linguistic usage is. Jurisprudence not only points out what such common factors are, it discusses how probative each one is and how they relate one to another.

3. THE SUBJECT-MATTER OF JURISPRUDENCE

The specific subject-matter of jurisprudence consists of the arguments whereby valid legal rulings are derived.

4. JURISPRUDENCE IS "THE LOGIC OF LEGAL UNDERSTANDING"

Like logic, jurisprudence is about what all correct thinking has in common. However, logic applies to all thinking, whereas jurisprudence is specific to the derivation of legal rulings.

5. THE IMPORTANCE OF JURISPRUDENCE IN THE PROCEDURE OF DERIVATION

The author emphasizes the importance of this discipline for the practical jurist, the practitioner of legal understanding. Somebody who knows the sources of the law – notably Qur'ān and tradition – thoroughly but cannot think about them systematically is not an adequate jurist. But neither is somebody who understands the method theoretically yet does not command the sources in detail.

6. JURISPRUDENCE IS TO LEGAL UNDERSTANDING AS THEORY IS TO APPLICATION

The preceding section should not be taken to mean that a jurist who knows jurisprudence can mechanically look up pertinent passages in the sources of law and thus painlessly derive particular valid legal rulings. For example, ascertaining common linguistic usage was mentioned as a methodological concern. Such ascertainment is not a self-realizing process, it is something the legal practitioner must think about carefully in each case.

7. THE INTERACTION OF JURISPRUDENTIAL THOUGHT AND LEGAL-UNDERSTANDING THOUGHT

We have seen that jurisprudence and legal understanding depend upon one another. Such is the case historically as well. Originally there was no separate field of jurisprudence, but as more and more specific derivations of legal judgments were made by practical jurists, naturally a desire to seek out the common threads in the mass of legal materials grew, and once that tendency was underway it had an impact upon the thinking of the practical jurists. Meanwhile the age of divine legislation was becoming more remote for everybody, which meant that general methods became necessary to address cases which were not originally obscure but had become so by mere lapse of time. There is a Sunni-Shī'ī distinction to be made in this matter. Until 260/874, the Twelver Shīᶜa had authoritative Imams who could pronounce legal judgments by inspiration and therefore the problem of growing obscurity and the need for a general methodology was less urgent. Nevertheless, there are discussions in early Shīᶜī books that point forward to the later discipline of jurisprudence.

8. THE PERMISSIBILITY OF THE PRACTICE OF DERIVATION

Fundamentally, everybody agrees that it is permissible to derive legal rulings. Some Shīʿī jurists, however, have seemed to say otherwise, because they rejected a certain older understanding of the word *ijtihad*, namely a specifically Sunni view that a jurist may "exercise *ijtihad*" in the sense of appealing to personal judgment as a distinct source of legal rulings. There is no difficulty if *ijtihad* is understood more generally to mean that the jurist must apply conscientious effort and the word thus describes the manner of his thinking and not a supposed source of it.

2. Substantiating Arguments

9. THE LEGAL RULING: DEFINITION AND SUBDIVISIONS

A divine-legal ruling is God's legislative act for the regulation of human life. The Qur'ān and hadith indicate what this ruling is, but they are not the ruling itself. The early equation of legal rulings with the divine discourse itself was not accurate: a ruling is the purport of the discourse. Similarly, it was not accurate to restrict legal rulings to divine discourse "about legal agents." The broader and proper criterion is that a legal ruling should be about regulating human life. Institutions like marriage and property are not directly about legal agents, but nevertheless divine discourse about them reveals legal rulings, since the institutions are aimed at regulating human life.

9a. The Division of Legal Rulings into "Injunctive" and "Declaratory"

An injunctive ruling is one directly addressed to individual behavior, like the prohibition of wine. A declaratory ruling is one related more indirectly to individual behavior, as for instance a ruling about marriage from which the man's individual duty to support his wife arises. Every declaratory ruling, however, invokes an individual duty (and therefore an injunctive ruling).

9b. Categories of Injunctive Rulings

Injunctive rulings are classified as:

1. mandatory
2. encouraged
3. prohibited
4. discouraged
5. permissible (neither encouraged nor discouraged).

Part Two – Topics Investigated by Jurisprudence

10. DIVISION OF THE DISCUSSION ACCORDING TO TYPES

The main division of types of derivations in the discipline of jurisprudence was mentioned at the outset. It is that between (a) derivations of a legal ruling that can invoke a substantiating argument, as opposed to (b) cases in which that better way is not possible and one must have recourse to a procedural principle. An example of the latter is a case where the legal ruling is derived by use of the priority of exemption, which says (approximately – details will be discussed below) that in cases of global doubtfulness about what the legal ruling ought to be, the procedural argument should be for a ruling of permissiblity. The author says "The difference between a procedural principle and a substantiating argument is that the principle does not firmly grasp the actual state of things but only defines a practical duty toward it." [In this sentence "capture" (*'aḥraza*) is etymologizing the word here rendered "substantiating."]

11. THE COMMON ELEMENT IN BOTH TYPES OF DERIVATION IS ASSURANCE

One crucial factor is common to both types of legal-ruling derivation, namely the probativity of assurance on the part of the legal agent. Assurance, like knowledge, must count as evidence if there is to be any legal science.

There are two reasons why assurance must be taken to have evidential bearing on the derivation of the ruling. (1) Acting against orders in [mistaken] good faith is a valid defense against a charge of disobedience, and (2) acting in acknowledged bad faith merits punishment. These two situations are referred to as exculpatoriness and inculpatoriness respectively. [The second is very prominent in the discussion of so-called "non-specific knowledge" below.]

The derivation of the ruling would not be "effective" if it disregarded the assurance of the legal agent. Indeed, we are told that "the jurist's act of derivation is of itself no evidence" and would also have no practical consequence unless the probativity of assurance is assumed. Not only is it a mistake to deny this view, but affirming it is fundamental to the whole field. Denying it virtually amounts to denying that any knowledge or any assurance can be probative. The scholar who is deriving a ruling about somebody else's legal situation under judgment is himself in a legal situation under judgment when doing so, and if his knowledge and assurance are legally irrelevant, then the whole discipline of jurisprudence simply could not exist, even if it did nothing but work directly from Qur'ān and tradition and never ventured on more rationalistic arguments (such as those used in the procedural principles).

The author acknowledges in so many words that all this is an appeal to reason. We are told that God Himself could not refuse to exculpate somebody who in good faith thought he was complying with His commands. God could, if He chose, warn the legal agent that this assurance is in fact mistaken, but that is a different question altogether.

[Plainly, then, ignorance of the law might seem to count as an excuse in this system. Yet the author's words for "knowledge" and "assurance" (*ʿilm* and *qaṭʿ*) are very strong, so there is in effect a notion of invincible ignorance here. In any case, there is no intention to apologize for people who take no pains to find out what the law demands.]

12. TYPE I: SUBSTANTIATING ARGUMENTS

A substantiating argument arrives at assurance about the legal ruling, and therefore the jurist must rely on it whenever available. When such an argument is not available, the ruling is known only defectively. Nevertheless the Lawgiver has authorized the use of certain types of deficient argument as if they were assured, as for instance in the case of traditions related by a single, but reliable, source. When it is unclear whether the Lawgiver has authorized the use of a certain sort of deficient argument, the presumption is that He has not. The maxim has it that "[ordinary] conjecture is not probative, only extraordinary conjecture counts as assured argument," the extraordinary kind being that specifically authorized by the Lawgiver.

12a. Subdivision of the Discussion

A substantiating argument consists of two parts: (1) a prooftext, an actual basis in revelation (Qur'ān and the speech or action of an infallible person, explicit or implicit), and (2) the reasoning process applied to it. The first is further divided into (a) verbal and (b) non-verbal argument. The principle that silence implies assent may apply in the non-verbal case.

The jurist has a threefold duty as regards the revealed basis: (a) to understand it correctly according to its prima-facie meaning, (b) to recognize that it is applicable and must be relied upon, and (c) to be sure that it comes from the Lawgiver. These three duties will now be discussed in that order.

13. DIVINE-LAW EVIDENCE

13a. Part One: Verbal Divine-Law Evidence

13a1. Signification

13a1a. Introduction. The author proposes to begin with a general discussion of semantics.

13a1b. About "Designation" and "Linguistic Connection". When we hear a word, we think of the thing the word means. This motion of the mind from word to meaning is called signification. The word is a "signifier," the thing is a "signified." Signification is, loosely speaking, a cause-and-effect connection.

But how did this cause-and-effect connection originate? Some say the connection is intrinsic, but that must be wrong, because you have to learn a particular language for this word-to-meaning transition to happen. The cause-and-effect relationship was established by whoever invented a particular language: these people may be called "designators," the verbal expressions, "the designated," and the thing meant, "that for which the designated stands."

But how did this designation process work? There never was any intrinsic connection between word and meaning, and the designator cannot have simply willed the connection into existence. The answer lies in the human habit of association. So prone are we to associate ideas, that sometimes a single conjunction makes two things come to mind almost simultaneously.

Some designations may have been onomatopoeic (like "ouch!"), but for the most part the designators were doing the same thing parents do when they name a child and more or less the same thing we all do when we make up a mnemonic for ourselves.

A crucial feature of designation (once established) is that it is spontaneous and unreflective. This has a bearing on when language is being used literally.

13a1c. About "Use". When one utters an expression in order to make someone think of the meaning with which designation has connected it, one is said to use it. There are three important components here, (1) the verbal expression ("what is used"), and (2) the meaning it is supposed to make a listener think of ("what it is used for"), and (3) one's deliberate intent that the listener should so think. There is also a word-meaning association happening in the speaker's mind, of course, but that is automatic and unconscious. The author discusses and rejects a theory that one single expression cannot be deliberately used in two distinct senses because of this unselfconsciousness on the speaker's part, which is conceived as involving a sort of "absorption" of meaning by the utterance.

13a1d. "Literal" and "figurative". An expression is used literally ("truly") when it entirely agrees with the meaning established by designation. When it only partly agrees, when it is in some respects like the designated meaning but not identical with it, the use is said to be figurative. When an expression is used figuratively, there is usually something contextual in the utterance itself which makes this clear.

13a1e. Figurative May Become Literal. Usually there is something in the context for this to happen, but sometimes figurative usages develop and no longer require such a clue each time. The author calls this sort of thing, our "dead metaphor," "automatic designation" as opposed to the "specifying designation" of the original designator when the expression was first coined.

13a1f. Language Distinguishes "Substantive" and "Relational" Meanings. [Three parts of speech are distinguished in traditional Arabic grammar, nouns (including adjectives), verbs, and "particles," *i.e.*, everything else. Thinking mainly of prepositions and conjunctions, one may consider a particle is a relation-indicator. Literally translated, the terms used here are "nominal" and "particulate."]

Substantives (nouns) have meaning in themselves, relational words do not; on the other hand, substantives do not indicate relationships. The verb is twofold, materially a substantive, but formally a relation-word. Jurists [as opposed to grammarians] consider that there exist only substantive meanings and relational meanings, but say that a finite verb has both kinds together.

13a1g. The Shape of the Sentence. The sentence as such has a relational meaning, specifying the connection between subject and predicate.

13a1h. Complete and Incomplete Sentences. The author explains the difference between what we would call attributive phrases ("the learned scholar") and sentences proper ("the scholar is learned") in terms of the former being "integrating" and the latter "non-integrating." A complete sentence must be of the second type.

13a1i. The Lexical Signified and the Assentable Signified. Recall that "signified" and "signifier" relate more to ordinary communication, whereas "designation" is about the coinage of words. Designation creates the linguistic cause-and-effect link called signification. Signification happens automatically: a native speaker of a language cannot hear a sentence of it as only so much noise – the meaning springs to mind at once. However, this is purely a lexical affair, an association made inside the system of designations. Real-world or assentable signification requires that a human speaker intends for this assentable signification to happen in a listener's mind. The author cites talking in one's sleep and even "the result of the friction of two stones" as cases where the listener can find a conceptual significance in the sounds but there is no assentable signification present. [Parrots *etc.* would presumably be another example.] The difference is the element of "intention in use" mentioned above. There is also an element called " intention to be serious" that is absent in jokes. When both elements of intention are present we have assentable signification. The speaker does not merely want us to understand his meaning, he wants us to agree with it. Obviously this sort of signification is extralinguistic.

13a1j. Declarative and Performative Sentences. In addition to "intention in use" and "intention to be serious" there is another sort of intentionality, the sort that distinguishes a performative sentence ["I offer to sell you this book for a dollar"] from a declarative one ["I sold you this book for a dollar"], even if the two are formally identical, as is the case in Arabic for the verb "sell/sold." The author is concerned to refute the view that such a sentence does not involve any additional element not discussed in the previous section. He clinches his argument by pointing out that performative sentences are usually recognized to be different from declarative ones in purely linguistic ways: we could tell which is which even with somebody talking in his sleep who doesn't at all intend anything he says.

13a1k. The Significations That Jurisprudence Considers. The author distinguishes general and special significations, mentioning the imperative form of the verb as an instance of the former, and the concept "charity," of the latter. Jurisprudence is only concerned with general significations, and detailed discussions of five such are provided.

1. The Imperative Verb. The great issue is whether an imperative is always absolutely mandatory or sometimes only advisory. There are jurists who insist on the first view, but the author disagrees. He acknowledges that absolute command is the paradigmatic case. Our out-of-context reaction to any imperative is to accept it as absolute command, but in context it can mean encouragement to do such-and-such as well as a rigorous demand. He expressly calls this a figurative usage in line with his definition above.

2. The Prohibitive Verb. We find exactly the same treatment here as between utter prohibition and mere discouragement.

3. Absolute Expression. Unrestricted (but not explicitly generalized) utterances are taken to be general. (The examples here contrast "Respect your neighbor" with the restricted "Respect your Muslim neighbor.") It is presumed that "the wisdom of the speaker" has deliberately omitted to restrict the universality of the application of the expression.

4. Explicit Generality. Generality can also be explicitly marked with words like "every." The author takes the view that the Arabic definite article with a plural noun is not an explicit marker of generality, but others have disagreed. [Everybody agrees that its use with a singular noun can be generalization. "Man is vile" would require "*the* man" in Arabic.]

5. The Conditional. Conditional sentences with "when" or "if" imply two different legal rulings. If an action is conditionally prohibited (or mandatory or whatever – cf. §9b above) when the condition obtains, then it is not prohibited (or whatever) when the condition does not obtain. The negative side of the matter, with the ruling reversed when the condition is not realized, is implicit, but this negative side is taken by the jurists to be present in every case. Yet that rule applies only to a spelled-out conditional sentence, not to an incidental epithet, to "Respect your neighbors if they are Muslims" but not to "Respect your Muslim neighbors."

13a2. Probativity of the Prima Facie

A divine-law argument cannot concern itself only with lexical or conceptual signification. The jurist must discuss it in terms of assentable signification to make out what the Lawgiver intended.

At this point we invoke the assistance of "the prima facie" in two senses. (1) We rely upon the prima-facie sense of the revealed text, the sense that comes to mind at once. (2) We rely upon the prima-facie intention of the Lawgiver that the text should be so understood. The jurists agree that (2) affords an assured argument. This approach, "the priority of the prima facie," does not mean that nothing is ever understood figuratively rather than literally, since we have seen that the figurative can become literal by commonly accepted usage.

When there seems to be a conflict between the two, the prima-facie sense presented by the Lawgiver in context outweighs considerations of what is most common in language generally. Nevertheless it is crucial that the jurist be aware of the latter.

The evidence that such is the proper procedure is twofold: (1) This is how the Companions of the Prophet and the Imams interpreted, as may be seen from studying the way they acted. (2) Those who are infallibly guided saw in their time that this was the procedure in use and they did not reject it. Therefore the "priority of the prima facie" constitutes assured argument.

13a2a. "Probativity of the Prima Facie" Applied To Verbal Evidence. The author considers three situations that may arise when attempting to find an argument based on the principle of the probativity of the prima facie:

1. The revealed utterance has only one possible meaning.
2. It has two or more equally likely possible meanings (whether due to homonymity or to figurative language).
3. It has two or more possible meanings, but one is in context clearly the most likely.

The first case is unproblematic and affords a substantiating argument directly. The second case is unresolvable – no argument can be discovered on this basis. [This does not mean that there is no answer, only that it cannot be based on (this sort of) argument. A second-best invocation of the "procedural principles" is necessary.]

In the third case, our author of course concludes that the obviously right meaning should be relied on and the alternative(s) ignored. But since there is a possible alternative, he treats this case more elaborately, in terms of:

13a2b. "Conjunct" and "Disjunct" Contexts. By a context he understands not a whole passage, but the specific clue in it that makes plain how to take a multivalent expression. Such a clue must exist given that one interpretation is clearly to be preferred. It may be either in the immediate vicinity of the multivalent expression (making it a conjunct context) or at a distance (if it is a disjunct context.) [In this book, the latter seems to mean that the contextual clue is in a different tradition from the one with the multivalent expression in it.]

The author's example is instructive: he assumes the multivalent expression is "Respect every poor person" with a context of "Respect every poor person except sinners." Since the latter is more explicit and detailed, it must be preferred over the theoretically possible interpretation of respecting everybody poor without exception. [This sort of interpretive hesitation is not what we understand by "figurative," – nor exactly our "multivalent" either, perhaps – but it is strictly in accord with the broader definition of the term so translated, just as an imperative used to mean encouragement rather than dictation was specifically called "figurative." See §13a1d. and §13a1k. above.]

13a3. Establishing the Source

Jurisprudence is also concerned with general procedures for establishing that a given utterance does in fact come from an infallible person. [This discussion is all concerned with traditions.]

Four methods are discussed.

1. Transmission on a wide scale. If a large number of transmitters agree about the attribution of the saying, ordinary rules of thinking make us accept the attribution. There is no need for this commonsensical procedure to be authorized by an infallible person as per §12 above.

2. Consensus and prevalence. If a uniform consensus or heavy preponderance of jurists have relied on an utterance as inspired and affording an argument, then it is safe to rely on it. But this consensus or prevalence must demonstrably exist, otherwise the jurist is relying on worthless supposition.

3. Common practice of the religiously observant. This is in effect the consensus of the whole community as opposed to that of the jurists. What all the pious have always done is the right thing to do. *Ergo*, the tradition that tells them to do so is sound. However, there

are reservations and restrictions on this principle which the author does not spell out in so brief a survey.

4. A reliable single-person account. A tradition narrowly transmitted may be relied on if it comes from a person of good character. Relying on it is a deficient argument in the terms of section §12. The defect is made good by Qur'ān 49: 6, "O you who believe, if a sinner comes to you with a report, look into it carefully...." The author argues *a fortiori* that the reports of non-sinners are to be cherished even more highly. The author stresses that this procedure relies on the Lawgiver's authority, not on reason or on the integrity of the transmitter in his own right.

14. NON-VERBAL ARGUMENT IN DIVINE LAW

Argument may be based on the non-verbal behavior of an infallible person. Actions performed by such a person must be regarded as "permissible" or "encouraged" (see §9b). Actions pointedly abstained from by such a person must be regarded as "prohibited." These actions are established by the same rules about tradition we just discussed for verbal argument.

The maxim "silence implies consent" applies to such cases. The author distinguishes between specific tacit consent (when somebody is related to have done such-and-such in the presence of an infallible person without being rebuked) and generalities like the conduct of reasonable people. The "probativity of the prima facie" discussed already is yet another instance of such generalized tacit consent. This principle is different from the consensus of the religious community in item (3) of the previous section. That consensus rests ultimately on revelation, whereas the conduct of reasonable people comes about only from reason and not from piety.

The real authority appealed to in such a case is not reason as such, however, but an infallible person's tacit endorsement of what reason says.

15. RATIONAL ARGUMENTS

15a. The Study of Rational Connections

There are a number of connections between things that reason apprehends, as for example contrariety, cause-and-effect, and also "antecedence and subsequence" or hierarchical subordination. Such rational connections allow us to make valid inferences. They apply to divine-law rulings as well as to everything in the world of nature.

15b. Subdivision of the Discussion

Rational connections in the sphere of divine-law rulings exist between

1. one ruling and another ruling,
2. a ruling and its subject,
3. a ruling and its dependent object,
4. a ruling and its necessary preliminaries,
5. one internal part of a ruling and another, and
6. a ruling and the extralegal world.

The last item is described as referring to the logical consequences of the ruling, a topic to be postponed to a more advanced level.

15c. Rational Connections Between Different Rulings

15c1. The Polarity of Mandatory and Prohibited

One can perform two actions simultaneously, one mandatory and the other forbidden. That is no problem, because each part may be ruled on separately. It is logically impossible for one and the same act to be both mandatory and forbidden. However, the jurists hold that an act may be unitary in essence but at the same time be compound in respect of its legal categorization. An example of this would be performing mandatory ablutions with stolen water. The act is one, but the jurists must note that ablution is mandatory and misappropriation forbidden. There are two schools of thought on this point. (1) Some hold that the necessary difference in classification means that there are "really" two acts here, even though they cannot be separated. (2) Others insist upon the strict unity of the act. This difference is phrased in terms of holding "the (im)possibility of coexistence of obligation and prohibition." Our author prefers the second view. He argues that one's primary concern must be with the intention of the Lawgiver and not with the physical details of an act. The resulting "coexistence of obligation and prohibition" exists in the Lawgiver's mind and does not imply any logical contradiction in the natural world or in human conceptualizations, which are always based on the natural world.

15c2. Does Prohibitedness Require Invalidation of a Contract?

The answer is no. "Mandatory" and "forbidden" are contraries of one another, and so are "valid" and "invalid," but that does not make "forbidden" and "valid" contraries. "Forbidden" means that the Lawgiver does not want such a contract made, but nevertheless, once it is made, the ordinary legal consequences follow. This principle does not apply to acts of devotion, however, where the other party to the transaction is God Himself and the object of the act is to come closer to Him, which is impossible if one does what He forbids.

15d. Relations Between a Ruling and its "Subject"

[The subject of a ruling is not its subject-matter in the sense of prayer or contracts or inheritance or some such rubric, but more like its "matter" in the Aristotelian sense, the concrete stuff the form of the ruling is instantiated in.]

15d1. Promulgation and Actuality

At the time God revealed that pilgrimage to the Kaᶜba is "mandatory for anybody who can find a means to do it" [Q. III: 97], perhaps there was in existence nobody who actually could find the means. A divine-law ruling about the pilgrimage being mandatory has two aspects, the original promulgation of a divine-law injunction in general and the actuality or applicability of that promulgated injunction to particular persons. The divine injunction itself exists independently of whether it actually applies to anybody – its promulgation is one thing, and its actualization is quite another.

15d2. The Subject of a Ruling

The "subject of a ruling," in legal terminology, is what is necessary for there to be an "actuality" of the "promulgation" of the ruling in the sense just explained. In the example, it would be the actual existence of Muslims capable of undertaking the pilgrimage.

The relationship between the subject of a ruling and the ruling proper is somewhat like a cause-and-effect relationship. The actuality of its subject causes the ruling to concretely take effect.

This relationship is of general importance in jurisprudence. For example, the jurists have a maxim that the subject of a ruling cannot be a consequence of the ruling itself, since the subject must precede the actualization of the ruling. Hence there cannot be a ruling which has knowledge of that ruling itself as part of its own subject, since knowledge of the ruling must come after the ruling itself, whereas the subject of it must come before.

15e. Connections Between a Ruling and its "Dependent Object"

The "dependent object" of a ruling is the human behavior which it requires. Whereas the subject of a ruling must come before it, its dependent object must come afterwards. The actualization of the ruling brings into existence an obligation which then stands in a quasi-causal relationship to the dependent object of the ruling. Since this whole process must take place in the order indicated, it would be nonsense for the dependent object of the ruling to involve bringing into existence the subject of the ruling. Thus in the pilgrimage example, what is mandatory is making the pilgrimage if one is capable, not becoming capable of doing so.

15f. Connections Between a Ruling and its "Necessary Preliminaries"

Two different sorts of "necessary preliminaries" are distinguished. (1) Those upon which the dependent object of a ruling depends (like the travel involved in making the pilgrimage), and (2) those upon which the subject of the ruling depends (like the wealth required to be capable of making the pilgrimage). In the latter case, the existence of any obligation depends on these necessary preliminaries, but not in the former case, since there the ruling has already come into effect.

Case (1) is illustrated in terms of the relationship between ablution and prayer. The obligation to pray has no direct connection with ablution, which is a necessary preliminary for actually praying, not for being obliged to.

We have already seen that in case (2) there can be no obligation to perform the necessary preliminaries, since obligation arises only after the subject of the ruling is actualized. However case (1) is quite different: prayer having been established as mandatory, the *sine qua non* preliminaries for it (like ablution) are also mandatory.

There is a technical disagreement among jurists about exactly how the obligation to perform the necessary preliminaries arises in case (1). Some say that the divine law proper makes only the dependent object itself (like prayer) obligatory and that it is reason which works out that the necessary preliminaries (like ablution) are therefore indispensable. Others hold that the divine law itself mandates both the dependent object of a ruling and its necessary preliminaries. Our author takes the first view, arguing that since reason can discover the secondary obligation, it is not necessary that the Lawgiver should expressly mandate it.

15g. Connections Within a Single Ruling

The obligation arising from a ruling (and its dependent object) may consist of a series of distinguishable acts and not just one; such is the case with prayer. If the whole series is mandatory, so are all the parts of it, but each part is said to involve "incorporated obligation" as opposed to the "independent obligation" of the whole series. Unless all the incorporated obligations are complied with, the independent obligation is not complied with. This maxim entails that if there exists a valid impediment to performance of any one of the incorporated obligations, the others need not be performed: the legal agent is dispensed from the independent obligation as a whole.

Two cases must be distinguished. If the independent obligation stands alone, it simply ceases to be obligatory because of the impediment and that is that. But what if the independent obligation was itself a necessary preliminary to the dependent object of some quite different obligation? (In the author's example, a skin disease would be a valid impediment to washing one's face as part of the series of acts constituting ablution, and one would be dispensed from the other parts of ablution also. But where does that leave one insofar as ablution is a necessary preliminary to prayer?)

Our author says that one is dispensed from the primary obligation as well. He considers the supposed parallel of a man becoming mute and therefore unable to perform the recitation which is an incorporated obligation of liturgical prayer and is therefore obliged to pray silently instead. The cases are not really parallel, however, because this silent prayer is not a part of the independent obligation of prayer, but an alternative to it specifically mandated by the Lawgiver.

3. Procedural Principles

16. INTRODUCTION

The exposition of the first type of derivation of a divine-law ruling, that based on substantiating arguments, has now been concluded. We turn to the second type, which bases itself upon procedural principles. This approach is resorted to only when no substantiating argument can be found and the proper ruling remains in doubt. Technically speaking, the procedural principles do not derive the ruling itself, they only tell us how to cope in practice.

Consider smoking. Our author presumes that it is forbidden, but he cannot adduce a substantiating argument for his opinion. After failing to find one, the first procedural question he raises is whether he needs to exercise precaution in this case. It is the role of the procedural principles to decide whether precaution is necessary.

[The author differs from others who reverse the order of the first two principles, beginning with "exemption" rather than with "precaution." Furthermore, his third principle of "the inculpatoriness of non-specific knowledge" replaces a much simpler idea of "optional choice" (*takhyīr*) found in other Twelver jurisprudence.]

17. THE BASIC PROCEDURAL PRINCIPLE

To understand about precaution, it is necessary to start from the very beginning and ask oneself what obedience to the divine law is grounded upon. The answer is reason, which perceives that God has a just claim to human obedience. It is reason that tells us in general to obey God, not God Himself. Mankind would have a general rational duty to try to obey God even if He had never specifically commanded anything. When an argument is not available to tell us with assurance what He has specifically commanded, we are in effect thrown back upon that duty as established by reason or natural religion. Accordingly, when substantiating derivation of a divine-law ruling is not possible, it is for reason to guide us. In fact, reason always guides us, since it of course tells us to obey what we know God has specifically commanded, but in the absence of such specific knowledge, reason suggests that we ought to take account of what God *may possibly* have commanded. The name of this rational account-taking is precaution.

The author says "In a fundamental way, whenever we consider prohibition or obligation possible, the source of law is the exercise of precaution."

To be excused from the reason-imposed duty of precaution, we must adduce a divine-law argument that precaution may be dispensed with in the case at hand.

So says our author. Other jurists have argued, however, that where firm knowledge of the specific ruling is unavailable, there can *ipso facto* be no duty of obedience on the part of a legal agent. They appeal to our common-sense notion that it is wrong for a master to punish his slave for not doing what the latter was never explicitly ordered to do. The author rejects this line of argument, because mankind does not stand vis-à-vis God as ordinary slaves stand to ordinary masters.

18. THE SECONDARY PROCEDURAL PRINCIPLE

Having announced that precaution is fundamental, the author nevertheless says "The basic principle [*sc.* precaution] is inverted by the ruling of the Lawgiver into a secondary procedural principle – 'the priority of exemption' – which advocates the non-obligatoriness of precaution."

To "invert" precaution into exemption requires (*cf.* §12) a substantiating divine-law argument, which is at once provided. The author refers to a tradition about Muḥammad saying "My religious community are relieved of that which they do not know."

The upshot is that "we adhere to exemption when we are in doubt," whether in doubt about a ruling or the subject of a ruling.

19. THE INCULPATORINESS OF NON-SPECIFIC KNOWLEDGE

19a. Introduction

In addition to specific knowledge (the complete absence of doubt) and "doubt" in the sense of being entirely at a loss, there exists an intermediate condition of non-specific knowledge. For example, you may know for sure that at least one of your brothers is making the pilgrimage and yet not know which one of your brothers it is.

The proper linguistic formula for non-specific knowledge is "I know that EITHER ... OR ...." [This seems from the treatment as a whole to be always *inclusive* OR – either X or Y or possibly both, but definitely not neither.]

From the viewpoint of jurisprudence, specific or detailed knowledge means that a substantiating argument can derive a ruling, and sheer blank ignorance means that "the priority of exemption" applies. Invocation of the other procedural principles is reserved for cases of non-specific knowledge.

19b. Inculpatoriness of Non-Specific Knowledge

An example: how does one pray at noon on a Friday? With the ordinary prayers as on other days of the week [since the Imam is absent], or with the special Friday prayers? Undoubtedly one or the other is mandatory, but which one?

It would be an abuse to apply "the priority of exemption" to such a case and argue that since we are in doubt, we have no obligation to do either. Unaided human reason sees that that would be an abuse, a pretending not to know what we do in fact know. God does not permit us to act in a way so contrary to our own knowledge.

Since the secondary principle of exemption does not apply, the primary principle of precaution must. Precaution advises us to perform both the ordinary prayers and the special Friday prayer. When we thus go out of our way to make sure that we are meeting our known obligations, the jurists technically speak of our "assured compliance."

19c. Resolution of Non-Specific Knowledge

We have seen that the linguistic formula for non-specific knowledge is "either X or Y [or maybe both]." When we gain more knowledge about such a situation, it is usually knowledge about X alone or Y alone, and the result of our additional knowledge runs something like "definitely X, but I haven't a clue about Y." That is to say, one component moves up from non-specific knowledge to knowledge proper, but the other component moves downwards into complete doubtfulness. In terms of jurisprudence, X becomes a matter we now have a substantiating argument about, and Y becomes a matter which the "priority of exemption" legitimately applies to.

19d. Occasions of Hesitation

We can be in doubt about what kind of doubt we are in, unsure whether or not we have any non-specific knowledge. The problem can arise in conjunction with composite obligations, such as when we know that nine items are mandatory but are uncertain whether or not to include a tenth item. Juristically speaking, this means we do not know whether exemption or precaution applies. There are two schools of legal thought about how to proceed, one advising precaution and the other exemption. Our author favors exemption.

20. THE PRESUMPTION OF CONTINUITY

When we are uncertain about something at the moment but were sure about it at some time in the past, we are to presume that nothing has changed. The argument for this is the reliable tradition that Ja^{c}far aṣ-Ṣādiq [the sixth Imam of the Shī^{c}a] said "Certainty cannot be destroyed by doubt."

20a. The Previous Condition of Certainty

The previous state of affairs we were sure about (and are to presume continues) may be about the law or about the facts, *i.e.*, either about a ruling or about the subject of a ruling (*cf.* §15d2. above). Some jurists hold, however, that the presumption of continuity applies only to fact, not to law. Our author challenges them to adduce a context (*cf.* §13a2b.) that requires the tradition cited in the previous section to be understood in so restricted a sense.

20b. Doubt Concerning Persistence

There are two different reasons why we may be unsure that a previously known state of affairs persists. Either it was a *status quo* that of itself naturally would persist (but we are not certain whether or not some external intervention has changed it), or else it was a *status quo* we knew would expire. An example of the latter is the daytime fasting in Ramaḍān, daytime being obviously not perpetual. Some jurists hold that the presumption of continuity does not apply to cases of the second type, but once again our author rejects restriction of the continuity presumption.

20c. Unity of the Subject and the Continuity Presumption

The continuity presumption does not apply to cases where there is doubt about whether the substance of a thing (as opposed to its accidents) persists.

4. Conflict of Arguments

21. THE CONFLICT OF ARGUMENTS

That concludes the discussion of the various methods of deriving a divine-legal ruling. It remains to be explained how one proceeds when different methods point towards different conclusions. There are three cases:

1. Two substantiating arguments clash.
2. Two procedural principles clash.
3. An argument clashes with a procedural principle.

21a. Conflict Between Substantiating Arguments

21a1. Conflict of Verbal Substantiating Arguments

1. There cannot be two clear and assured prooftexts which point to different rulings of the five types in §9b, since the Lawgiver does not contradict Himself.

2. Yet a clear and assured prooftext may conflict with the prima-facie sense of another and a resolution is possible by taking the second in a figurative sense. This is illustrated by a case where a prohibition is understood to be intended as recommendation rather than absolute command because there is a plain prooftext calling the same act permissible. A general rule is formulated for cases of this sort according to which the statement of permission [ordinarily in the indicative mode], which does not contain this linguistic ambiguity between stronger and weaker interpretations, is to be preferred.

3. When the subject of the ruling in one prooftext is more specific than that in the other, the former is to be preferred. It is taken as a "context" (in the special sense discussed above) for understanding the more general one. We distinguish between [positive] specification and [negative] restriction, but both take precedence over another prooftext which is more generally expressed, whether or not some word like "all" is actually present. At the same time, the general formulation remains probative outside the range of the specification or restriction.

4. The subject of the prooftext for one ruling may be rendered impossible by the other text, as when "Pilgrimage is mandatory for the capable" encounters "A debtor is not a capable person" and we

conclude that the debtor need not make the pilgrimage. In such a case, the second is said to "overrule" the first. In this case, as well as (2) and (3), the resolution is arrived at by "reconciliation based on common usage," referring to common usage of language.

5. When neither prooftext is clear and assured, and neither can be treated as a context for the other, one may not use either, because there is no basis to prefer either. [We must presumably use the procedural principles to handle the case. As mentioned in §11, in no situation do we simply decide we cannot decide, although we may not actually "substantiate" the divine-law ruling.]

21a2. Other Situations of Conflict

An assured rational argument cannot conflict with a substantiating divine-legal one because of the infallibility of the Lawgiver. The author's most unambiguous state of "rationalism" runs: "Not only does dogmatic belief propound this truth, it is demonstrated by induction based on the divine-law texts and by study of the assured data of the Qur'ān and the sunna, for they altogether agree with reason. There is nothing whatsoever in them that conflicts with the assured dictates of reason."

Verbal substantiating arguments are preferred over any other sort.

An assured rational argument is preferred over a merely presumptive one based on the prima-facie sense of a prooftext. The Lawgiver cannot be in conflict with reason, so He *must* have intended something other than the prima-facie sense of the unclear text.

When two non-verbal arguments clash, both cannot be assured. Sometimes it is possible to decide which one is assured.

21b. Conflict Between Procedural Principles

The main case here is the conflict when exemption and the presumption of continuity both seem to be applicable. The latter is dispositive and overrules exemption, because it eliminates the subject of any ruling that exemption is permissible by eliminating the element of ignorance or doubt demanded by the prooftext "My religious community are relieved of that which they do not know." (*cf.* §18)

21c. Conflict Between the Two Types of Argument

Strictly speaking, a procedural principle can never conflict with a substantiating argument, because the latter has already attained to assurance, whereas use of the principles is warranted only where there exists some element of doubt or ignorance.

Nevertheless, there exist also deficient arguments (*cf.* §12) which fall short of being assured and are only presumptive. In the case of a single-source tradition (which is a deficient type of argument), are we to treat it as substantiating because the Lawgiver has vouched for it ("Certainty cannot be destroyed by doubt," *cf.* §20) [even though reason does not make it seem anything better than presumptively true to us], or may we invoke the principle of exemption because "presumptive" of course means that we remain to some extent in doubt? We must do the former and treat the deficient argument as substantiating, relying on the Lawgiver's word rather than upon reason.

Glossary

Absolute expression (*'iṭlāq*)
An expression which is not restricted (but also not expressly generalized) is taken to be general, on the assumption that the speaker deliberately rejected the idea of restricting it. This is called "the CONTEXT of wisdom," taking the wisdom of the speaker as the contextual clue to the intended sense.

Account (*khabar* pl. *'akhbār*)
Usually means a HADITH. See under TRADITION.

Actuality (*fi'liyya*)
The term is used in roughly the Aristotelian sense. The actuality or actualization of a ruling is the fact that it actually applies to some particular legal agent, any elements of conditionality (and thus potentiality) in the prooftext having been realized. See also SUBJECT OF [A RULING].

The author also refers to the actuality as *maj'ūl*, "that which was promulgated." See also PROMULGATION.

Analogy (*qiyās*)
A Sunni SOURCE OF LAW rejected by Twelver Shī'īs like the author.

Argument (*dalīl* pl. *'adilla*)
Literally, "indicator" or "indication." "Proof" is rather too strong, and "evidence" is rather misleading, since the reference is always to concepts and argumentation, never to physical or material evidence. Like RULING, "argument" can, by a sort of shorthand, mean the PROOFTEXT on which a DERIVATION is based.

When used without any modifier, ARGUMENT almost always means a SUBSTANTIATING ARGUMENT.

Articulation, divine (*khiṭāb*)
Address in the second person. God's address to mankind.

Assent, assentable (*taṣdīq*, *taṣdīqī*)
The adjectival form is used, not to indicate that a speaker is positively soliciting a hearer's agreement, but rather that he or she intends (and the hearer takes) what is said as inviting a judgment of being true or false.

The contrary of it is *taṣawwurī*, CONCEPTUAL, which describes a situation where the speaker or hearer understands the meaning of an UTTERANCE but has not yet attached any real-world relevance to it. For a speaker's meaning to be assentable, there must be two elements of volition on his part, the INTENTION IN USE (namely, of language, to communicate) and the INTENTION TO BE SERIOUS. The former is absent in a case such as talking in one's sleep, the latter in cases of joking or irony. ASSENT has both a subjective side and an objective one, but the former predominates. The term might be glossed as the speaker's intention that the hearer take what he says to be applicable to the real world.

Used non-technically, *taṣdīq* can mean that the hearer thinks an utterance is in fact true, or at least that he thinks the speaker is not lying.

Assurance (*qaṭ'*)
The firm subjective assurance of the LEGAL AGENT about either the facts or the law is always a material circumstance which the JURIST must consider.

Assured (*qaṭ'ī*)
The opposite of *zannī*, PRESUMPTIVE. See also DOUBT.

Chain (of transmission of hadith) (*'isnād*)
The ascription of a HADITH or other narrative on the basis of a chain of authorities, preferably uninterrupted, to an original witness.

Clear Statement (*bayān*)
Speech making apparent what is in the mind. In particular, the clear speech or statement sent by God to mankind through a Prophet.

Common usage (*'urf* [n.] *'urfī* [adj.])
In this text it almost always means the common usage of language.

Conceptualization, conceptual (*taṣawwur, taṣawwurī*)
The framing of a meaning in the mind without any implication one way or another about its truth value in external reality. The term is derived from *ṣūra* "picture, image, form, concept."

Conditional [particle] ([*'adāt ash-*] *sharṭ*)
Conditional clauses always imply two rulings, a positive and EXPLICIT (*manṭūq*) one when the condition is met, a negative and IMPLICIT (*mafhūm*) one when it is not met.

Conduct of reasonable people (*sīra 'uqalā'iyya*)
In law, *'āqil* [pl. *'uqalā'*] means a person of sound mind. The conduct of reasonable people means a general inclination among reasonable people to a specific form of conduct. The universal practice of the human race in a particular matter is EVIDENCE unless there has been a RULING to the contrary from an INFALLIBLE PERSON. See further under REASON.

Conjecture (*ẓann*)
An ARGUMENT based on conjecture is not PROBATIVE and is deficient, unless there is a perfect SUBSTANTIATING DIVINE-LAW ARGUMENT that THE LAWGIVER has specifically ruled that such a type of DEFICIENT ARGUMENT is to be accepted and accounted ASSURED. The SINGLE-

SOURCE ACCOUNT is an example of a type of ARGUMENT that has been externally vouched for in this way.

Linguistically, conjecture is related to PRESUMPTIVE (*ẓannī*), the pair contrasting with ASSURANCE and assured (*qaṭʿ* and *qaṭʿī*) as well as with DOUBT and doubtful (*shakk* and *mashkūk*).

Conjunctive context (*qarīna muttaṣila*)
A CONTEXT (in the technical sense) which occurs in the same passage as the ambiguous expression it contextualizes. The alternative is *qarīna munfaṣila*, a disjunctive context. In practice, the latter expression seems to mean that the clue to understanding the ambiguous expression is found in a different source of the law.

Consensus (*'ijmāʿ*)
Agreement. Agreement of either the overwhelming majority of the Muslims, or of the JURISTS of one's group on a legal RULING, the validity of a TRADITION, *etc.*

Context (*qarīna*)
Technically used, a context is not the whole passage in which an ambiguous phrase appears, but rather a particular clue that shows how the ambiguity is to be resolved. The ambiguous phrase is called *dhū/dhāt al-qarīna*, literally "the owner of the context," but better rendered in English as "the contextualized."

Continuity, presumption of (*istiṣḥāb*)
The procedural principle which holds that a previously known state of affairs or ruling is presumed to continue to obtain.

Declarative sentence (*jumla khabariyya*)
A sentence that states facts independent of the speaker's wishes and therefore is not PERFORMATIVE.

Declaratory ruling (*ḥukm waḍʿī*)
A RULING which does not impose an individual obligation directly but rather sets up an institution (such as marriage or private property) from which a variety of individual obligations subsequently flow. See

also INJUNCTIVE RULING. There is no DECLARATORY RULING which does not involve one or more injunctive rulings.

Deficient argument (*dalīl nāqiṣ*)
A deficient argument is one that leads only to conjecture as opposed to ASSURANCE, or so it would seem to REASON. Nevertheless, if there is a perfect (*kāmil*) SUBSTANTIATING DIVINE-LAW ARGUMENT showing that such an ARGUMENT has been ruled acceptable, it is to be used in DERIVATION on the same basis as an ASSURED ARGUMENT. See further under CONJECTURE.

Dependent object [of a ruling] (*muta'allaq* [*al-ḥukm*])
The concrete duty of the LEGAL AGENT as imposed by a RULING. Given a ruling that one must make the pilgrimage, the dependent object of that ruling would be (among other things) one's traveling to Mecca. Our author stresses that the dependent object always comes after the ruling has become an ACTUALITY, whereas the SUBJECT OF THE RULING always comes before.

Derivation, to derive (*istinbāṭ*)
To elucidate a DIVINE-LAW RULING on the basis of relevant ARGUMENTS and SOURCES OF LAW.

Designation (*waḍ'*)
In the discussion of semantics, designation is parallel to SIGNIFICATION, except that it refers to the original coining of words as opposed to their regular use subsequently.

Both terms are differently construed in Arabic than in English: the designator/signifier is a person, and he is said to designate/signify the word to its meaning. Hence "the designated" or "the signified" is the word, not the meaning. The latter is literally called "the designated to" or "the signified to." In the case of the last phrase, the word "significance" will be used here, but unfortunately there is no "designance" in English.

Since all of this falls strictly within the LEXICAL realm, it is still only the mental meaning, not the external thing meant, that is involved. See further the discussion of CONCEPTUAL and ASSENTABLE.

The foregoing refers to *waḍʿ taʿyīnī*, "specifying designation," the coining of a word by a specific individual. There is also *waḍʿ taʿayyunī*, "self-specifying designation," which refers to the process whereby a FIGURATIVE meaning becomes LITERAL.

Detailed Knowledge (*ʿilm tafṣīlī*)
The ordinary sort of knowledge; full knowledge as opposed to NON-SPECIFIC KNOWLEDGE.

Discretionary Opinion (*istiḥsān*)
In ruling on a question, turning away from comparable questions. In Sunni jurisprudence, what the JURIST by his REASON approves of.

Dispensation (*rukhṣa*)
An indulgence granted by God to a LEGAL AGENT as a facilitation. A RULING of indulgence such as the shortening of prayer for travelers and the like.

Divine law (*sharīʿa* [n.] *sharʿī* [adj.] *sharʿan* [adv.])
What God wants mankind to do, taken comprehensively. In the present discussion only DIVINE LAW is at issue, and therefore plain "law" and "legal" will often stand as abbreviations for "divine law" and "divine-legal." *Sharīʿa* stands in partial distinction from *fiqh*, LEGAL UNDERSTANDING, although in modern usage the two are often interchangeable.

Dogmatic belief (*ʿaqīda*)
Creed, articles of faith, dogma.

Doubt, doubtful (*shakk*, *mashkūk*)
The author distinguishes PRIMARY DOUBT, from NON-SPECIFIC KNOWLEDGE.

Engagement (*ishtighāl*)
See under PRECAUTION.

Enjoin, injunction (*taklīf*)

(a) God's imposition of a legal obligation through which a person acquires a duty.

(b) Legal capacity, *cf.* LEGAL AGENT.

Evidence (*ḥujja*)

This term almost always means dispositive evidence and the word is often translated "proof." It is etymologically connected with PROBATIVITY.

Exculpatoriness (*mu'adhdhiriyya*)

The RATIONAL view that a LEGAL AGENT who believes with ASSURANCE that he is complying with a RULING of THE LAWGIVER – even though he is in fact mistaken – may not be blamed or punished.

Exemption (*barā'a*)

The PROCEDURAL PRINCIPLE which assumes that, when a RULING is subject to PRIMARY DOUBT (as opposed to cases of NON-SPECIFIC KNOWLEDGE), there is no duty imposed on the LEGAL AGENT.

Explicit (*manṭūq*)

The opposite of *mafhūm*, IMPLICIT. See under CONDITIONAL.

Fifth, tax of one-fifth (*khums*)

Religious tax of twenty per cent on net profits owed to the IMAMS. In their absence, Twelvers pay it to the leading legal authorities. Half of it is meant for the religious establishment, and half for the believers, primarily the needy, especially the needy among the family of the Prophet (who cannot benefit from the alms tax). It is mentioned here both as a tax on inheritances and on mines.

Figurative [use of language] (*majāz* [n.], *majāzī* [adj.])

Any USE of an expression that involves a meaning not identical with that given it by DESIGNATION is called FIGURATIVE. When an expression is used figuratively, there is always a CONTEXT which shows us that the designated meaning is not what was meant.

The idea is broader than English "figurative." In this book it appears most frequently in conjunction with IMPERATIVE and PROHIBITIVE verb forms: absolute command is taken to be the LITERAL meaning, whereas it is figurative to take such forms in a weaker sense as only encouragement or discouragement.

By a process called SELF-SPECIFYING DESIGNATION, a figurative expression may become literal, which means that it can be used in a sense different from that of its original SPECIFYING DESIGNATION without any need for a CONTEXT every time that newer sense is intended.

Friday prayer (*ṣalāt al-jum'a*)
Among the Twelver Shia, the permissibility of the special prayer said at noon on Friday in the absence of the IMAM is disputed.

Generalization, generality (*'umūm*)
The distinction between *'āmm*, "general," and *khāṣṣ*, "specific," is fundamental to the way Islamic JURISTS and experts in JURISPRUDENCE analyze language. This distinction is important in connection with ABSOLUTE EXPRESSION as well as with express generalization.

Hadith (*ḥadīth*)
See under TRADITION.

Hierarchical subordination (*ta'akhkhur rutbī*)
A RATIONAL connection wherein B is secondary to A only in respect of rank without being caused by A or subsequent to A in time. One case of this relationship is SUCCESSION IN EXISTENCE.

***Ijtihad* (*ijtihād*)**
The exercise of DERIVATION of a RULING by a JURIST. More narrowly, the authority to derive rulings for the Muslim community as a whole. There is assumed to be a chain of qualified jurists extending back to the time of the IMAMS. From the seventh/thirteenth century, such qualified jurists are called MUJTAHIDS among the Twelver Shia.

Imam (*'imām* pl. *'a'imma*)
(1) For all Muslims, the leader of congregational prayer.

(2) Again for all Muslims, the head of the Muslim community. Sunnis more often call this officer a caliph.
(3) For Shīʿīs, a specific hereditary line of heads of the community descending from ʿAlī and Fāṭima, the Prophet's son-in-law and daughter respectively. The Twelver Shia, to which the author belongs, recognize a line of twelve such Imams (counting ʿAlī), the last of whom did not die but went into *ghayba*, "occultation," or absence, in the third Muslim century. All these IMAMS are INFALLIBLE PERSONS.

The issue about the FRIDAY PRAYER at noon mentioned several times in this work is whether the IMAM, in sense (3), must be visibly present in the world so that he can lead it, or whether somebody may act as his deputy, or whether there is no legitimate deputy, in which case it may be forbidden to pray the special Friday prayer.

In the legal realm, the sixth IMAM, Jaʿfar aṣ-Ṣādiq [died 148/765] is especially important. The school of law to which the author belongs is sometimes called Jaʿfarī by the Sunnis and listed as a fifth school together with Ḥanīfīs, Mālikīs, Shāfiʿīs and Ḥanbalīs. When the author refers to his own religious community as a whole, he calls it the *'Imāmiyya*.

Imperative [verb form] (*'amr*)
Literally, "command." The great issue about imperative verb forms is when they are to be taken to be peremptory and when only as recommendation. The former use is considered LITERAL, the latter FIGURATIVE. See also PROHIBITIVE.

Implicit (*mafhūm*)
The opposite of *manṭūq*, EXPLICIT. See under CONDITIONAL.

Impure, impurity (*najis*, *najāsa*)
See under PURE.

Inculpatoriness (munajjiziyya)
The view of REASON that a LEGAL AGENT cannot be excused for acting contrary to a RULING of THE LAWGIVER when he knows it with ASSURANCE.

Indeterminate (*mujmal*)
An UTTERANCE the meaning of which is unclear; something that is the object of NON-SPECIFIC KNOWLEDGE.

Indication (*'amāra*)
An ARGUMENT that is PRESUMPTIVE, but valid.

Infallible person (*ma'ṣūm*)
A person protected by God from speaking error and committing sin. See under IMAM.

Inference (*istidlāl*)
Seeking an appropriate argument (*dalīl*). Reasoning, argumentation, demonstration, conclusion, inference, deduction.

Injunctive ruling (*ḥukm taklīfī*)
A RULING which imposes an obligation directly upon an individual LEGAL AGENT.

Specifically, the ruling that a particular act is categorized as one of the following:

- mandatory (*wājib* [adj.] / *wujūb* [n.])
- encouraged (*mustaḥabb / istiḥbāb*) [also *mandūb / nadb*]
- permissible (*mubāḥ / 'ibāḥa*)
- discouraged (*makrūh / karāha*)
- forbidden (*ḥarām / ḥurma*).

These are the five sorts of *'aḥkām taklīfiyya*, injunctive rulings, appropriate to be used in a legal ruling about any human act. Other schools than the author's, while maintaining the five categories, use different terminology. Many JURISTS make further subdivisions within each of these five rulings.

In addition to injunctive rulings, there are *'aḥkām waḍ'iyya*, DECLARATORY RULINGS.

Integrating [phrase/clause/sentence] ([*jumla*] *indimājiyya*)
Integrating phrases or clauses (as opposed to non-integrating, *ghayr indimājiyya*, complete sentences) are explained below in connection with RELATIONAL MEANINGS.

Intention (*niyya*)
The precept established by the Prophetic saying, "Actions are to be judged according to intentions" is almost always fundamental to LEGAL UNDERSTANDING.

Intention in use (*'irāda isti'māliyya*)
See under USE and ASSENT.

Intention to be serious (*'irāda jiddiyya*)
See under USE and ASSENT.

'Iqāmah (*'iqāma*)
The second call to prayer which is usually given by the prayer leader in the mosque (or by the individual when praying in private) before each of the five daily prayers. It marks the true beginning of the prayer.

Jurisconsult (*mujtahid*)
Practitioner of IJTIHAD.

Jurisprudence (*'uṣūl al-fiqh*)
"Knowledge of the common elements in the procedure of deriving rulings of the DIVINE LAW." (Bāqir aṣ-Ṣadr's formal definition at page 31.)

Another Twelver Shī'ī specialist in JURISPRUDENCE considers the discipline to be the investigation of rules which have proved useful for deriving rulings.

Literally the expression means "roots of legal understanding." A traditional Twelver list of such primary sources for making a legal ARGUMENT runs 1. Qur'ān, 2. HADITH, 3. CONSENSUS and 4. REASON. Among the Sunnis, the fourth item is usually *qiyās*, ANALOGY, rather than reason.

See further under SOURCE OF LAW.

Jurist (*faqīh*)
A practitioner of *fiqh*, LEGAL UNDERSTANDING.

The Lawgiver (*ash-Shāri'*)

God, or mediately, Muḥammad and the other prophets who brought a divine message, and other INFALLIBLE PERSONS.

Legal agent (*mukallaf*)

Literally, "one enjoined," *cf.* INJUNCTION.

The term is used two ways: 1. a person obligated by a particular RULING to perform that ruling's DEPENDENT OBJECT. 2. More generally, a person capable of being subject to a RULING, one who is, so to say "enjoinable," *i.e.*, adult, of sound mind, acting voluntarily, *etc.*

Legal understanding (*fiqh*)

(a) Human knowledge or supposition about *sharī'a*, the DIVINE LAW.
(b) Islamic law, a body of law as developed and understood by Muslims.

Necessarily this sense of the term allows for differences in human formulations of this body of law. (In modern usage, *fiqh* is often used interchangeably with *sharī'a*.)

Lexical (*lughawī*)

Pertaining to the sphere of a language, to a received system of DESIGNATIONS and SIGNIFICATIONS, without reference to the external world. *Cf.* the discussion under ASSENT. In practice, the language system involved is Classical Arabic.

Limit (*ghāya*)

This means a temporal limit, a deadline. In the discussion of CONDITIONAL sentences, it is to be distinguished from "delimit" or "define" (*taḥdīd*), which can refer to any sort of (de)limiting.

Linguistic connection (*'alāqa lughawiyya*)

The connection between an UTTERANCE and a specific meaning was originally established by DESIGNATION, and then a process of CONCEPTUAL association created the regular LEXICAL system of SIGNIFICATION.

Literal (*ḥaqīqī*)
The literal ("real") meaning of an expression is the one given it by DESIGNATION. When it is used in a way not identical with that, the USE is called FIGURATIVE.

Necessary preliminary (*muqaddama*)
Note that strictly speaking there are two sorts of necessary preliminaries that may be involved with a given RULING, (1) those preliminary to the SUBJECT OF THE RULING, and (2) those preliminary to its DEPENDENT OBJECT.

Non-specific knowledge (*'ilm 'ijmālī*)
The basic idea is knowing that either X is so or Y is so or both X and Y are so – but not knowing the details about X or Y taken separately with specific knowledge, nor yet being in PRIMARY DOUBT. The jurisprudential notion extends to cases with more than two alternatives, although none occur in the examples here.

Opinion (*ra'y*)
A Sunni SOURCE OF LAW rejected by Twelver Shī'īs like the author, insofar as it refers to personal opinion not based on a PROOFTEXT.

Optional choice (*takhyīr*)
This is the third PROCEDURAL PRINCIPLE in many other accounts of Twelver Shī'ī JURISPRUDENCE, standing where our author has the INCULPATORINESS of NON-SPECIFIC KNOWLEDGE. OPTIONAL CHOICE is said to obtain when we know that either X is so or Y is so but not both.

Overruling (*ḥākim*)
This word is a form of the verb corresponding to the noun RULING. When two lines of ARGUMENT conflict, it is applied to the one that is to be preferred, *i.e.*, the one that arrives at the jurist's final idea of what the applicable divine-law ruling is. The rejected ARGUMENT is *maḥkūm*, "overruled."

Passage (siyāq)
See under SEQUENCE OF SPEECH.

Performative sentence (*jumla 'inshā'iyya*)
A performative sentence, for Bāqir aṣ-Ṣadr, is any sentence that contains some element of intentionality on the speaker's part, including all IMPERATIVEs and PROHIBITIVEs. "It shall happen" he would call performative, whereas "It will happen" would be what is commonly called a DECLARATIVE SENTENCE.

Practical position (*mawqif 'amalī*)
A position as to what the LEGAL AGENT should do in practice (as opposed to a theoretical position.)

Precaution (*iḥtiyāṭ*)
The PROCEDURAL PRINCIPLE which consists in going out of one's way to make sure one complies with possible as well as with certainly known divine injunctions.

The term *ishtighāl*, ENGAGEMENT, is synonymous.

Presumption of continuity (*istiṣḥāb*)
The PROCEDURAL PRINCIPLE which holds that a previously known state of affairs or RULING is presumed to continue to obtain.

Presumptive (*ẓannī*)
The intermediate alternative between *qaṭ'ī*, ASSURED, in one direction, and *mashkūk*, DOUBTFUL, in another.

Prevalence (*shuhra*)
Literally "fame." The term applies to HADITHS that are very widely (but not universally) transmitted and agreed upon. Also, opinions within a school widely, but not universally, held.

Prima facie (*ẓāhir* [adj.] *ẓuhūr* [n.])
Literally, "external, immediately apparent." Our author, like most Muslim scholastic thinkers, assumes an ultimately Aristotelian correspondence theory of truth, and therefore that the apparent is probably the real.

Primary doubt (*shakk badawī*)
Complete uncertainty, as opposed to the partial doubtfulness associated with NON-SPECIFIC KNOWLEDGE.

Priority (*'aṣāla*)
Cf. under *'aṣl*, SOURCE OF LAW.

Probative, probativity (*ḥujjī, ḥujjiyya*)
Evidential, tending to show. Validity. Quality as a proof. *Cf.* EVIDENCE.

Procedural principle (*'aṣl 'amalī/qā'ida 'amaliyya* pl. *'uṣūl/qawā'id 'amaliyya*)
General principles which the jurist resorts to only when DERIVATION of a RULING with a SUBSTANTIATING ARGUMENT is impossible. Specifically, 1. PRECAUTION, 2. EXEMPTION, 3. the EXCULPATORINESS of NON-SPECIFIC KNOWLEDGE, and 4. the PRESUMPTION OF CON-TINUITY.

The adjective could be rendered "practical," but the immediate reference is not to the PRACTICAL POSITION of the LEGAL AGENT but to the technical procedure of the jurist.

Prohibitive [verb form] (*nahy*)
The issue with prohibitives (negative commands) is exactly the same as with IMPERATIVES: are they meant literally as absolute forbidding, or figuratively as no more than discouragement?

Promulgation (*ja'l*)
The promulgation of a RULING is its original establishment by THE LAWGIVER, as opposed to the ACTUALITY of a ruling, which refers to its becoming incumbent upon a specific LEGAL AGENT after the SUBJECT OF THE RULING has come to exist.

Prooftext (*naṣṣ* pl. *nuṣūṣ*)
Literally, "explicit designation." A quotation from Qur'ān or reliable *hadith*, preferably one that is completely unambiguous, with no possible second meaning, however far-fetched or improbable. Also, the entirety of the Qur'ān and the reliable hadith as revelation.

Pure, purity (*ṭāhir*, *ṭahāra*)

The discussion about the ritual PURITY of water in connection with the PRESUMPTION OF CONTINUITY assumes that we know that any sufficiently large quantity of water is intrinsically PURE. A dog (which is intrinsically IMPURE) cannot pollute the Euphrates. In addition to things like these which are always in the same state of (IM)PURITY, there are neutral things which may be polluted by contact with something intrinsically IMPURE, in which case they become "extrinsically impure" and can pass on the taint to other neutral things.

Reason, rational (*'aql* [n.], *'aqlī* [adj.], *'aqlan* [adv.])

Sometimes better translated "intellect." Often the phrase "according to reason" appears alongside "according to divine law," *shar'an*. Reason is understood to be necessary to acquire belief. Reason is in some measure necessary for the JURIST to draw conclusions from PROOFTEXTS, although the authority of these texts rests on divine PROMULGATION accepted as part of belief.

A rational argument, *dalīl 'aqlī*, can yield a SUBSTANTIATING ARGUMENT for a RULING, as for example that the NECESSARY PRELIMINARIES to something mandatory are themselves mandatory.

At times, *'aql* can best be translated "common sense," as in conjunction with the CONDUCT OF REASONABLE PEOPLE.

Relational meaning (*ma'nā ḥarfī*)

Literally "pertaining to a particle," a particle in Arabic grammar being any word that is neither a substantive (noun or adjective) nor a finite verb. Jurists consider that particles have no SUBSTANTIVE MEANING in themselves but express relations between other substantive meanings. Particles have relational meanings only. Finite verbs have a relational meaning, formally considered, and at the same time a substantive meaning, materially considered.

In addition, jurists attribute a relational meaning to the pattern (*ṣīgha*) of the basic sentence of predication on the model of "'Alī is an Imam," which in Arabic is the juxtaposition of two nouns without any explicit particle or finite verb signifying a relational meaning. This attribution is necessary because it is held that a complete sentence (*jumla tāmma*) must be non-integrating (*ghayr indimājī*) as opposed to a mere phrase or clause (*jumla nāqiṣa*) which is integrating (*indimājī*) and non-integration may express an (external) relationship. "The learned jurist" is integrating and expresses only a single (though compound) substantive meaning, whereas "The jurist is learned" expresses two substantive meanings and the relational meaning obtaining between them.

Reliable-source account (*khabar ath-thiqa*)
A hadith transmitted by one deemed to be trustworthy as a transmitter of accounts about INFALLIBLE PERSONs. See also SINGLE-SOURCE ACCOUNT.

Response (*fatwā*)
A JURIST's formal legal opinion in reply to an inquiry, the *responsum* of Roman law.

Restrict(ion) (*taqyīd, qayd*)
When an UTTERANCE does not involve ABSOLUTE EXPRESSION, it is either restricted on the negative side or else explicitly generalized.

Ruling (*ḥukm* pl. *'aḥkām*)
(a) The behavior God ENJOINs upon the LEGAL AGENT.
(b) A judgment as to what God either assuredly or presumptively enjoins.
(c) Loosely, the PROOFTEXT which the JURIST uses to DERIVE a ruling.

Rulings are divided into two categories, INJUNCTIVE and DECLARATORY.

Self-evident (*badīhī*)
That which comes to mind spontaneously.

Self-specifying designation (*waḍ' ta'ayyunī*)
A secondary development in language whereby a FIGURATIVE USE of the originally designated UTTERANCE becomes a LITERAL USE in its own right. See under DESIGNATION.

Sequence of speech, passage (*siyāq*)
"Context" in the ordinary English sense. See also CONTEXT.

Signification, to signify (*dalāla*)
The utterance-meaning transition in the minds of language users. Signification follows in the wake of designation, the original coining of LEXICAL items. The Arabic usage of these terms is discussed under DESIGNATION. Here are the actual forms for "signify":

- *dalāla* – signification, to signify
- *dāll* – signifier, person who signifies
- *madlūl* – signified, utterance to which a significance is assigned
- *madlūl lahu* – "signified-to," significance, meaning to which an utterance is assigned

This is the same family of words that contains *dalīl*, ARGUMENT, but with a specifically semantic application. In addition this word cluster is used in a completely non-technical sense, *i.e.*, "indicate." The basic verb can therefore mean "argue for" (in law) and "signify" (in semantics) and also plain non-technical "show."

Single-source account (*khabar al-wāḥid* pl. *'akhbār al-'āḥād*)
A HADITH transmitted by one or a few people in each generation of a chain of transmission, but a hadith that lacks WIDE-SCALE TRANSMISSION. Such a hadith is open to suspicion of collusion, but nevertheless, in the absence of any other PROOFTEXT, it is to be used by the JURIST when the transmitters are reliable sources. Appealing to the single-source account is an example of a DEFICIENT ARGUMENT.

Source of law (*'aṣl* pl. *'uṣūl*)
Literally "root," as contrasted with "branch(es)," *far' / furū'*. For the JURIST, a "root" is a valid point of departure in making a legal argument. JURISPRUDENCE is therefore the "roots of legal understanding," the name of the subject of this book. That phrase usually becomes "principles of law" or "principles of jurisprudence" in other English discussions. Many accounts of the subject (but not this one) are centered around a list of such points of departure. Bāqir aṣ-Ṣadr

implicitly has such a list – Qur'ān, SUNNA, CONSENSUS, REASON – but he defines his subject inductively or abstractly as the study of common elements in valid DERIVATIONs of RULINGs without starting from a list.

Aṣl is also used in a quite different way that may be technical but is not really technical in law. One says "the root of X is Y" to mean that Y is the default assumption or general rule about how to handle cases of type X, what to do about X when there is no known reason to treat it specially.

The standing of the "root," *'aṣl*, as something prior in the process of derivation to the "branch," *far'*, is called *'aṣāla*, PRIORITY. In some cases this term can be translated "legal presumption."

Specifying designation (*waḍ' ta'yīnī*)
The original coining of a linguistic expression. See under DESIGNATION.

Subject [of a ruling] (*mawḍū'* [*al-ḥukm*])
This term means neither the person subject to the ruling nor the subject-matter of the ruling, in the sense of marriage, or inheritance or the like, but the whole state of affairs that must exist for a RULING to achieve ACTUALITY (over and above its original PROMULGATION). When every element of conditional or contingent application in the PROOFTEXT has been realized, the subject of the ruling is actualized, which means that some specific LEGAL AGENT is now ENJOINED to perform the DEPENDENT OBJECT of the ruling. To cite the author's frequent example, since pilgrimage was made incumbent only upon those who could afford it, the existence of a particular Muslim who is able to afford it is technically called the subject of a ruling that he must make the pilgrimage.

Substantiating argument (*dalīl muḥriz* pl. *'adilla muḥriza*)
An ARGUMENT is a substantiating one when it arrives at the correct DIVINE-LAW ruling with ASSURANCE. There are two cases: (1) a *kāmil*, "perfect," substantiating argument derives the divine-law ruling with an assurance that even unaided REASON can recognize, whereas (2) a *nāqiṣ*, DEFICIENT ARGUMENT may not seem to reason to achieve

assurance, yet it is equally as good in LEGAL UNDERSTANDING, since an INFALLIBLE PERSON has vouched for it. The JURIST who wants to use a deficient argument must be able to adduce a perfect substantiating argument to show that some infallible person has in fact vouched for that particular sort of deficient argument.

Substantive meaning (*ma'nā ismī*)
Literally "pertaining to a noun or substantive." A substantive meaning is intelligible in isolation but it expresses no RELATIONAL MEANING. Nouns (a category which in Arabic grammar includes adjectives) have only substantive meanings. Finite verbs have both a (material) substantive meaning and a (formal) relational meaning.

Succession in existence (*tasalsul fī l-wujūd*)
The RATIONAL connection of what has been called "logical dependency," whereby one thing is secondary and subordinate to another without being either subsequent in time to it or caused by it. Another name for this connection is HIERARCHICAL SUBORDINATION.

Sunna (*sunna*)
The sunna comprises everything known about INFALLIBLE PERSONS that gives guidance for human conduct, including their words, their deeds and that to which they have given TACIT CONSENT.

Tacit consent (*taqrīr*)
A legal ARGUMENT can be based on the tacit consent of an INFALLIBLE PERSON who sees an action or situation and does not object. This principle applies also to generalities like the CONDUCT OF REASONABLE PEOPLE, which, by virtue of the tacit consent of an infallible person, is a SUBSTANTIATING ARGUMENT.

Tradition (*ḥadīth* or *khabar* pl. *'akhbār*)
The body of accounts transmitted from generation to generation since the days of the INFALLIBLE PERSONS whereby we have knowledge of the SUNNA. A hadith which cannot be challenged by any of the tests established in traditional hadith criticism is called

"sound," *ṣaḥīḥ*. A transmitter of hadith who is reputed to be of good character is called a "reliable authority," *thiqa*.

Use [in communication] (*istiʿmāl*)

A LEXICAL expression is "used" when it is uttered intentionally. There are two issues to be mentioned here: (1) basic *'irāda istiʿmāliyya*, INTENTION IN USE, *i.e.*, use of language to communicate at all, and (2) *'irāda jiddiyya*, INTENTION TO BE SERIOUS. If both these elements are present, the UTTERANCE contains ASSENTABLE as well as CONCEPTUAL SIGNIFICATION.

The JURIST presumes that both intentions are always present in the PROOFTEXTS he works with, which may sound not worth mentioning, considering from Whom they come, but it is a canon of interpretation actually appealed to, although rather indirectly. The threefold duty of the jurist as set out at page 58 involves

1. verifying that the prooftext comes from Him,
2. deciding what He meant by it (*sc.* its conceptual signification), and
3. considering "the probativity of that signification and that prima-facie meaning and the mandatoriness of reliance upon it."

The last item is about the assentable significance of the prooftext. There would be no PROBATIVITY in the signification of the prooftext and no reason to prefer the PRIMA-FACIE sense of it and no mandatoriness about relying upon it unless the prooftext had an assentable significance, and having one requires that both intent to use and intent to be serious be attributed to THE LAWGIVER.

Utterance (*lafẓ pl. 'alfāẓ*)

Sound with CONCEPTUAL SIGNIFICATION but not necessarily possessing ASSENTABLE signification.

Wide-scale transmission (*tawātur*)

Transmission of a HADITH by many persons in every generation, as opposed to a SINGLE-SOURCE ACCOUNT.

Ẓihār form of "divorce" (*ẓihār*)
An oath formula whereby a man separates himself from a wife by saying "You are to me like the back of my mother." It is a pre-Islamic Arab institution which continued but was disapproved of and required an act of expiation to undo.

Arabic Terms Mentioned in the Glossary

'adāt ash-sharṭ	conditional particle
'adilla	arguments
'adilla muḥriza	substantiating arguments
'aḥkām	rulings
'aḥkām taklifiyya	injunctive rulings
'aḥkām wad'iyya	declaratory rulings
'a'imma	imams
'alāqa lughawiyya	linguistic connection
'alfāẓ	utterances
'amāra	indication
'amr	imperative verb form
'aqīda	dogmatic belief
'āqil	person of sound mind
'aql	reason
'aqlan	according to reason
'aqlī	rational
'aṣāla	priority
'aṣl	root, principle, starting-point
'aṣl 'amalī	practical principle
'aṭrāf	alternatives (of non-specific knowledge)
badīhī	self-evident

barā'a	exemption
bayān	clear statement
dalāla	signification (semantics)
dalīl	argument
dalīl 'aqlī	rational argument
dalīl muḥriz	substantiating argument
dalīl nāqiṣ	deficient argument
dāll	signifier (person who uses a sign)
dhihn	mind (intellectual, not emotional)
dhū/dhāt al-qarīna	the contextualized
faqīh	jurist
far'	branch, application
fatwā	response
fi'liyya	actuality (of a ruling)
fiqh	legal understanding
furū'	branches, applications
ghāya	time limit
ghayba	occultation (of Twelfth Imam)
ghayr indimājī	non-integrating
ḥadīth	hadith, tradition
ḥaqīqī	literal
ḥākim	overruling
ḥalāl	permitted (*cf. mubāḥ*)
ḥarām	forbidden, prohibited
ḥujja	evidence
ḥujjī	probative
ḥujjiyya	probativity
ḥukm	ruling
ḥukm taklīfī	injunctive ruling
ḥukm waḍ'ī	declaratory ruling
ḥurma	forbiddenness
'ibāḥa	permittedness
iḥtiyāṭ	precaution
'ijmā'	consensus

ijtihād	ijtihad
'ilm 'ijmālī	non-specific knowledge
'ilm tafṣīlī	detailed knowledge
'imām	imam, prayer leader
indimājī	integrating
'iqāma	commencement of prayer
'irāda isti'māliyya	intention in use [language]
'irāda jiddiyya	intention to be serious
ishtighāl	engagement *cf. iḥtiyāṭ*
'isnād	chain [of hadith transmission]
istidlāl	to infer, inference
istiḥbāb	to encourage
istiḥsān	discretionary opinion
isti'māl	to use, use
istinbāṭ	to derive
istiṣḥāb	presumption of continuity
'iṭlāq	absolute expression
ja'l	promulgation
jumla 'inshā'iyya	performative sentence
jumla khabariyya	declarative sentence
jumla nāqiṣa	incomplete sentence
jumla tāmma	complete sentence
kāmil	perfect, complete
karāha	discouragedness
khabar	account, tradition, hadith
khabar al-wāḥid	single-source account
khabar ath-thiqa	reliable-source account
khiṭāb	articulation
khums	one-fifth (20% tax)
lafẓ	utterance
lughawī	lexical
madlūl	the signified (an utterance)
madlūl lahu	significance (a meaning)
mafhūm	implicit

maḥkūm	overruled
majāz	figurative use of language
majāzī	figurative [adj.]
maj'ūl	the promulgated *cf. fi'liyya*
makrūh	discouraged
ma'nā ḥarfī	relational meaning
ma'nā ismī	substantive meaning
mandūb	encouraged *cf. mustaḥabb*
manṭūq	explicit
mashkūk	doubtful, subject to doubt
mawḍū' al-ḥukm	subject of a ruling
mawqif 'amalī	practical position
ma'ṣūm	infallible person
mu'adhdhiriyya	exculpatoriness
mubāḥ	permissible
mujmal	indeterminate
mujtahid	jurisconsult
mukallaf	legal agent
munajjiziyya	inculpatoriness
muqaddama	necessary preliminary
mustaḥabb	encouraged
muta'allaq al-ḥukm	dependent object of a ruling
nadb	encouragement *cf. istiḥbāb*
nahy	prohibitive (verb form)
najāsa	impurity
najis	impure
nāqiṣ	deficient
naṣṣ	prooftext
niyya	intention
nuṣūṣ	prooftexts
qā'ida 'amaliyya	procedural principle
qarīna	context
qarīna munfaṣila	disjunctive context
qarīna muttaṣila	conjunctive context

qaṭ'	assurance
qaṭ'ī	assured (known with assurance)
qāṭi'	assured (knowing with assurance)
qawā'id 'amaliyya	procedural principles
qiyās	analogy
ra'y	personal opinion
rukhṣa	dispensation
ṣalāt al-jum'a	Friday prayer
shakk	doubt
shakk badawī	primary doubt
shar'an	according to divine law
shar'ī	pertaining to divine law
ash-Shāri'	the Lawgiver
sharī'a	divine law
shuhra	prevalence (of hadith)
ṣīgha	form, pattern (esp. grammatical)
sīra 'uqalā'iyya	conduct of reasonable people
siyāq	sequence of speech, passage
sunna	sunna
ṣūra	form, image, picture
ta'akhkhur rutbī	hierarchical subordination
ṭahāra	purity
ṭāhir	pure
takhyīr	optional choice
taklīf	injunction, to enjoin
taqrīr	tacit consent
taqyīd	restriction, to restrict
ṭaraf	alternative (of non-specific knowledge)
tasalsul fī l-wujūd	succession in existence
taṣawwur	conceptualization, to conceptualize
taṣawwurī	conceptual
taṣdīq	assent
taṣdīqī	assentable
tawātur	wide-spread transmission (of hadith)

ʿumūm	generality, generalization
ʿunwān	legal categorization
ʿuqalāʾ[ī]	[pertaining to] reasonable people
ʿurf	common usage
ʿurfī	pertaining to common usage
ʾuṣūl	roots, principles
ʾuṣūl al-fiqh	jurisprudence
ʾuṣūl ʿamaliyya	procedural principles
waḍʿ	designation (in semantics)
waḍʿ taʿayyunī	self-specifying designation
waḍʿ taʿyīnī	specifying designation
wājib	mandatory, obligatory
wujūb	mandatoriness, obligatoriness
ẓāhir	prima-facie [adj.]
ẓann	supposition
ẓannī	presumptive
ẓihār	oath of repudiating a wife
ẓuhūr	prima-facie meaning

Index

Note: Some subsections are listed in page order (rather than alphabetical order) to aid their coherence.